Diana Newlands was born in Woodford, a suburb of London, and has lived there all her life. This is not at all unusual in Woodford. There must be something about the place! She read English at Reading University and studied music at the Royal College of Music and the Guildhall School of Music, where she met her husband, Alastair.

She taught English for eight years before the birth of her son and daughter, was an examiner in London University Advanced Level English for seven years and at various times has worked as an accompanist and as an opinion research interviewer. She is a keen photographer, gardener and interior decorator, is Chairman of a local choir, the Crofton Singers, and a founder member of the Woodford Wells Ecumenical Church.

Diana, living alone now since Alastair's death in 2002, is part of a large close-knit family of relations and friends. They populate, and to a great extent inspired this book.

LIFE LINES

Diana Newlands

Life Lines

Vanguard Press

A CIP catalogue record for this title is
available from the British Library
ISBN 1 84386 139 9

*Vanguard Press is an imprint of
Pegasus Elliot MacKenzie Publishers Ltd.*
www.pegasuspublishers.com

First Published in 2004

**Vanguard Press
Sheraton House Castle Park
Cambridge England**

Printed & Bound in Great Britain

ACKNOWLEDGEMENTS

Thank you

to

Simon Cushman
Hara Olymbiou
Rebecca Seabrook-Tedd
Rachel Walls

four pupils of Bancroft's School, Woodford Green
for their illustrations

to Graham Welstead, Head of the Art Department and
Dr. Peter Scott, Head Master

and to my friend Mary Toms
and my son Gordon Newlands
for their additional artwork

IN MEMORY OF ALASTAIR

and dedicated to:

my mother Beryl in Eastbourne
our son Gordon in Balham
our daughter Ellie in Glasgow
my brother David in Theydon Bois
my sister Mary in Bristol
my brother Michael in Barbados

and to all the other friends and relations who have
shared the past nine years with us.

FOREWORD

The distraught figure arrived on the landing stage at Anderston Quay, Glasgow, just as the gangways were pulled up, ropes dropped, and the paddle wheels of the steamer *Waverley* began to churn. But then, the kindly – or prudent – captain, recognizing her as the mother of the then Commercial Director of the *Waverley*, went back and picked her up.

The passengers all crowded to one side of the boat, curious about the late arrival. She waved her hat at them and gave a bow as she came down the gangway. "What an entrance!" I said, "I'm envious".

That was my first meeting with Diana Newlands. I had come aboard for the trip to Greenock, to view the gathering of tall ships, and we got chatting. We talked about her home in Woodford, Essex, about public transport and shopping. We talked about the confusing instructions supplied with electrical apparatus. We talked about dictionaries, music, the theatre. And we talked about her husband, the operatic tenor Alastair Newlands, who had sadly suffered a major stroke.

This calamity was fairly recent and its effect on Diana's existence naturally extreme. The central line of communication in her life had been cruelly cut, and as an attempt to compensate she had begun to write regular letters about her thoughts and doings, which she copied and sent to a circle of relations and friends.

I cheekily asked if I might be included in the next mail-out. I was, and was delighted, and then somehow I got put on the regular list, and the letters were constantly entertaining, and in the end I suggested they should perhaps be edited and sent to a book publisher.

This is the result. Whilst keeping Alastair's memory alive through occasional references to a shared past, the letters deal perceptively with the present; the writer's encounters, surprises, joys and frustrations –and not just in Woodford.

Timothy West
May 2004

CONTENTS

September
Everything changes, doesn't it?

Everything changes, doesn't it? There used to be a high-class independent bakery at the bottom of the road. Cakes left over from the previous day's baking were sold off at half price, if you were lucky enough to get down there soon enough. The chocolate truffles were magnificent. The bakery turned into a travel agency for a while, but there was just one chap sitting in there with a telephone and a map of Sri Lanka on the wall. So he probably didn't pose much of a threat to the long-established Abbotts Travel opposite the post office. He seemed rather forlorn, I always thought, so I went in one day to do some photocopying. This was one of his sidelines. His machine took thirteen sheets of paper to copy my eight pages, so he didn't make much profit out of my visit, but we had a friendly chat. The inefficiency of his copier did rather undermine what little confidence I might have had in him to organise any foreign trip for us, even supposing we might ever again be able to contemplate such an adventure.

Anyway, he's gone now, and a genial entrepreneur from East London has opened up with second-hand office furniture, which he piles out on to the pavement each morning in good time to be appreciated by the occupants of crawling rush hour vehicles. I couldn't picture many local residents having a use for slightly worn ergonomic seating, even though he looks wonderfully comfortable lounging on it outside the shop in the Autumn sunshine, in gaps between customers. But within a week I was beginning to ask myself whether one of his astonishingly inexpensive four-drawer filing cabinets wouldn't quickly solve my mounting storage problems and contribute a giant leap forward in my determination to 'have things all sorted out' before Alastair eventually comes home from hospital in October. Correspondence with the Social Services, the Benefits Agency, the Local Health Authority, the Wheelchair Assessment Department, the Continence Advisory Bureau, Alastair's company Pensions Office, the Carers' Advice Centre...: there was paper everywhere. The genial entrepreneur delivered the filing cabinet after work today.

How does anyone ever manage without one? The filing cabinet has done a vacuum cleaner job. Paper has been sucked into it from shelves, cupboards and drawers throughout the house. All now in labelled files. The most important at the top. Letters from our son, Gordon, and our daughter, Ellie. Birth certificates. MOT and Car Insurance. Further down, domestic equipment guarantees, Barclaycard bills. A home for everything.

Near the bottom, at the back, there is now a file labelled 'Howlers'. I didn't realise I'd still got them. Dating back to my A Level English marking days. Hoarded lovingly. I wondered whether to rename the file 'Gems' since it contained much of the material that had shed sporadic shafts of (admittedly unintentional) joy across the long solitary red-biro hours of June and July, during my seven year term on the panel of examiners in the '70s. These 'gems' were not proffered by the cream of the candidates, those aspiring to an Oxbridge or any other Arts scholarship. Their creators may well have been 'doing' English because they couldn't think of anything else to do. It was probable that in most cases the examiner had more idea of what they were trying to say than they did themselves. But they were greatly valued. Far from mocking them, I found myself longing to send them a thank you letter, if I had known who they were. They had so enlivened my sometimes turgid task:

"Shakespeare has a great command of the language and all his verses are blank.... Antony has a weakness for passion.... Cleopatra is corrupt; she has affairs with important Romans.... Antony is pulled this way and the other at high frequency...He is angry and uses exclamation marks....Romantic love was considered to be a good idea in Shakespeare's day. A man who fell in love with a woman was expected to be sad and almost ill through thinking about her for much of the time. This is certainly unfashionable now....Even Enobarbus is drawn by Cleopatra's charisma, but he cannot put his finger on her fascination....Cleopatra's love for Antony is sincere; when he is away she obviously misses him and plays with the eunuch."

"Othello is an old Moor....he dismisses Iago during the marriage consummation ceremony....Iago is cooking a vengeance. He even tells Roderigo he is just out to feather his own pockets....Othello has to be admired for openly telling his wife the reason why he is murdering her.... later on he murdered himself by committing suicide....Othello ends his life with rhyming couplets....the closing line brings about the conclusion....the ending is a fate accomplis."

The candidates' reflections on Chaucer's pilgrims are also premier league stuff, but I'll save those for another day. Our copy of the 'Village Gazette' has just dropped on to the doormat. Unlike the freebie newspapers, which rarely break their journey between mat and bin, the gazette has the unique advantage of being ultra-local. It's a sort of one-man production by a chap in the next road. I think of him as our snooper-by-proxy; purveyor of useful gossip about who's starting up in business, who's folding, what specialist services or goods are available on our doorstep, who is campaigning about the bus delays or the fast-food litter in the borough flower beds. He's shamelessly pro the small businessman and, if not anti the big boys, then certainly suspicious of them. He was in good satirical form recently when Sainsbury's decided to 'sponsor' the shrubby roundabout in George Lane, just when Waitrose, co-incidentally, were laying the foundation stone of their grand new store on the old Gates Garage site about a hundred yards away. He concerns himself solely with the few square miles that make up our unassuming London suburb, of Woodford. Ilford might as well not exist. The same goes for Leytonstone and Walthamstow. We border them all as you know but they are *not* what the 'Gazette' is about.

So I suppose he and I have something in common: we find plenty to say about very little. Much ado about nothing really, especially in my case. Expect more of the same. With much love.

October
This week Grandma Beryl broke four toes

This week Grandma Beryl broke four toes, the front lawn yielded a fine crop of toadstools and our old friends Don and Annice came round with a load of freshly caught pollocks, straight from the sea off Cornwall. An unusually rich seam of news.

Grandma thought the last two stairs were only one; a common enough mistake, I dare say, though usually with less dramatic results. She now has plaster up to the knee. But she sounded no less perky than usual on the phone from Eastbourne this morning and in a hurry to stumble round the corner to the tearooms on the Marine Parade before her pals got there so she could have the crutches safely stowed out of sight. At last, Alastair has come home. How he would love to stumble even a few yards. The stroke was five months ago, on a Thursday. The day that changed our lives. Alastair had just returned from work and was in the middle of a three-point turn outside the house. I'd cooked a special meal that evening: sweet and sour chicken with rice and salad, and a fatless sponge topped with fresh strawberries. We'd been looking at a cookery programme the night before in which a chef magicked up a five-course feast in ten minutes and I'd thought to myself, "I've got a whole hour; I can easily manage a nice starter and a pud." But Alastair never ate that meal.

I haven't cooked a pollock before. To be honest I've never even heard of a pollock before. I checked it out in Chambers Dictionary. It's 'a marine fish belonging to the cod family, with a greenish-brown back, pale yellow sides, a white belly and a projecting lower jaw.' I thought we might grill one for our supper. Perhaps with some mushrooms. As for the toadstools, I think we must attribute them to the recent spell of heavy rain. The sort of rain that used to prompt Alastair to say he would apply for a mariner's certificate to enable him to navigate the M25 on his daily drive from South Woodford to High Wycombe. It's probably only because our house is up a hill that we aren't stacking sandbags in the front porch, like some unfortunate Kentish residents we heard about on the radio this morning. 'The wettest October for years.' Several of our umbrellas have sprung leaks. I don't know if you've ever tried to mend an umbrella but it's a pretty thankless task and you're more than likely to get a spoke in your eye. So it's better either to resign yourself to getting wet or to splash out on a new brolly.

Our son, Gordon, came for the weekend. The rain didn't deter him from a game of pitch and putt with his friend, Stephen. This morning Stephen phoned about his muddy boots. "Had he left them in my car after golfing with Gordon?" I groped around vainly in the garage for a bit, then returned to report in the negative. But meanwhile he'd remembered where he'd left them. He blushed down the line. But I told him not to worry. It made me feel so much better about the plastic detergent container. You know, the thing like a space capsule you "place in the heart of the wash." I'd lost track of mine. I'd tried the rubbish sacks, the kitchen cupboards, even the dark spidery places behind the Zanussi. A few days later I found it in the wardrobe up the leg of my joggers.

I did a spot of gardening at the front of the house this morning. Since no-one else looked likely to do it, I thought I'd clear away the straggling weeds and grubby-looking Michaelmas daisies that were clogging up the roots of the little kerbside tree the Council graciously planted outside our gate a year or two ago. I could just as easily have left a fork leaning up against the tree with a message for dog owners who regularly stand there inspecting the evening or noonday sky while their pets open their bowels, suggesting that they make use of their time to improve the environment while simultaneously abetting its pollution. But my biro chose that moment to run out, so I thought I'd do it myself. Various neighbours came by and offered their comments. On balance they were encouraging. I was regarded as public-spirited. Only one said what a shame it was to dig up the daisies. Anyone would think they were some sort of rare flora in an endangered habitat rather than just a convenient camouflage for canine crap. One lady progressed to more generalised, but related, themes: litter, flytipping, spitting in public, unwanted free papers. So it went on. Unexpected entertainment while I turned the soil, until she became so inflamed by her own oratory that I thought she was heading for some kind of seizure, and that I'd end up giving her the kiss of life amongst the weeds.

I've come to the conclusion I must have an honest face. Dave the butcher, Geoffrey the greengrocer, even Brad the garage mechanic: none of them worry if I turn up without my purse. "Pay tomorrow. Pay whenever. Don't come down again specially!" In my years of door-knocking market research, I was invited into homes of every shape and size. Ease of access varied: some residences required you to speak into a remote grid in a wall while staring, with what you hoped was a trustworthy smile, into an overhead camera. Others sat without pretension on the pavement so you could see straight down the hall and into the kitchen. A single step and you were in. I'll always remember the greeting of one Bethnal Green householder. She came to the door in curlers and carpet slippers, took one look at my clipboard and said,

"You know what you are don't you! A bloody nuisance! Get the kettle on! I'm going next door to get some tea bags."

I count it amongst the warmest of welcomes ever.

It wasn't much of a money-spinner, calling round to ask my "sample" what they thought of clingfilm or washing powder or weedkiller or whatever. That didn't take long. It was all the rest that took the time: the discussions about losing weight, keeping boyfriends, dealing with extravagant children, problems with breast-feeding, noisy neighbours, pipes that leaked. The topics were as varied as my "omnibus" questionnaires. Alastair called it my "ministry."

The question has often been put to me: "Are people very rude and dismissive when you turn up asking them for a bit of their day?" It may be that I was just lucky. But the fact is, I found little to connect the inhabitants of my suburban roads, streets, closes, crescents and avenues, whether they contained high-rise flats or detached desirable residences, with the graceless world presented in newspapers and glossy magazines or on television. Sometimes folk *are* busy, or plain "uninterested." And why not? That doesn't make them "rude." A huge proportion of "respondents" as we called them, were good-hearted, come-on-in people, more than ready for a chat, and entirely without the greed and cynicism and eagerness to cheat or milk the system that we are told so much about. The human race is OK! I loved knocking on its front doors. My guess is that the Interflora delivery lady probably has one of the sunniest views of humanity around:

"Bouquet for you, Mrs. Newlands... Mrs Smith... Mrs Jones."

How many retort,

"Not today, thank you."?

Whereas the bailiffs, debt-collectors and parking attendants probably regard humanity as an irredeemably bad lot.

January
Getting started is the worst bit

Getting started is the worst bit. Papering a wall, making a speech, writing a letter! I don't think I'm unusual in this. Watch a roomful of examination candidates open up and scan the question paper that they have anticipated and dreaded for months. The invigilator speaks. No hint of irony in his tone. It's more like indulgence, the offer of candyfloss at the funfair: "You may begin." If only they can! It's all very well for him to intone his fateful little iambi! He's settling down to a welcome hour or two of peace, enlivened by a cursory glance or two at the Times crossword or "Thompsons' Holidays." *They* are confronting their destiny! But once the pen begins to flow and the regurgitation process is under way, calm descends, pulses steady, brows cool, bowel contents coagulate.

The wise are wary and heed the instructions. They "read the questions carefully." For my part (I seem to have got started now) I think I may have to stop reading the newspaper. Can anyone ever smile again after a conscientious comb through an average day's reportage: earthquakes, floods, death, destruction? A young neighbour of ours experiences a grief that is unmistakably personal over the death of a child in, say, Puerto Rico or of a plane-load of holidaymakers in Tibet. He isn't just sad, as any of us might be. He mourns. He is impervious to consolation. I have a profound respect for his inconvenient humanity. Not for him the "What's the point of worrying about things you can't change?" attitude. There doesn't have to be a point for him. He shares the pain of others in distant anonymity.

I read somewhere that great comedians are often depressives in disguise: Hancock, Sellers, Milligan. It may be that the ability to extract true comedy from life depends crucially on the discovery that it's definitely no laughing matter. And even though I'm sure that you will all have grasped that tragedy and comedy are inseparable, and that people die at parties with a glass of champagne in their hand, I have nevertheless concluded that you would probably prefer letters that make you laugh rather than cry. Unless they be tears of laughter! So I'm grateful to the postman.

"Ah! Diana and Alastair must have received a letter announcing that they alone, of the inhabitants of Bressey Grove, are to be entered into a draw for a free trip to Disneyland...." That's what you're thinking. Or possibly "it's a letter from their bank staff saying that they are there to help them." Or even "an invitation to take a free copy of the F.T. daily for the next four weeks to enable them to keep abreast of how sentiment has been damaged on the Hang Seng by the falling dollar and by the 3.65 point drop on the Dow Jones following the recovery from flu of the President of Outer Mongolia."

But no, we had not received a letter. It was more a lack of letters. Let me explain. Before the night-carer goes at 7.30 a.m. I try to fit in a jog, which has now extended from one to several blocks. I couldn't help noticing this morning that all the post boxes had been turned into parcels. Not, as you might reasonably have expected, neat ones of the kind described in the Royal Mail pamphlet "Wrapping Up Well."

These were more like hastily bundled-up corpses, except that they were erect rather than supine. They had heavy-duty polythene sacks slung over their heads and torsos and were roughly tied with string but with no identifying tag or message. Of course, it *was* very early. My brain was probably still semi-dormant or it wouldn't have entertained for one moment the idea that presented itself: the idea that the violent winds and storms of the night had prompted some deeply responsible community-minded citizen to tuck them up snugly and protect their contents against an unprecedented inrush of sleet. The validity of this hypothesis diminished as the morning ticked on, the breakfast sunshine beamed in and the public-spirited polythene remained in place. I rang our local sorting office.

"Boxes? That's not us, that's Leyton."

"Leyton?"

"Yes. Leyton's boxes. South Woodford's sorting and delivering."

"How can you sort and deliver if we can't post?"

"It's like I say, it's down to Leyton."

"What's down to Leyton?"

"Leyton have lost the keys."

"The keys! What keys?"

"The keys to the boxes."

"Why? Who's got them?"

"That's what we don't know, isn't it!"

"But what about the letters posted yesterday?"

"Oh, they're all right. They're cleared. That's us. We're sorting and delivering."

I wondered how, if the keys were lost. But it seemed better to wish them a Happy New Year and hang up and make a cup of tea.

So now here we are at 10.20 a.m. and the Royal Mail van has just paused briefly beside the shrouded cadaver at the corner and driven off again. And the postman has delivered some routine mail: a belated Christmas thank you letter, a request to help save the South American rain forests and the gas bill. In short we are into the familiar January scene: the post-festive bathroom is exceptionally well stocked with aromatherapy essences and soothing balms, lovingly presented and gladly accepted and now serving as fragrant reminders of family activities at Christmas. Like the debates over whether my nephew, Richard, should be allowed maximum - or any! - points for "ground antelope's horn" as something beginning with G that you could put in a matchbox; or Grandad Harold's splendidly affectionate and seemingly sober "toast to absent friends" as we sat down to dinner on the day after Auntie Audrey's funeral; or the increasing ingenuity of family members when tracking down gifts at no more than £2 each, as per the family rules etc.

We have been "assessed". Subas, our social worker, has come into our life. We have "a package" of care. I am "covered" to work for two days each week. (MORI have been paying me to ask people questions for over twenty years! "Don't give up," they said, when I told them about Alastair's stroke. "Even if you only do one interview a month." It was what I needed to hear). So I went in to the office today and passed the whole of it talking to people about smog. Not a subject, you might think, to open up my horizons and bring light into my darkness. But it was good. A cup of coffee on one side, a telephone on the other. Little known but very worthy organisations all over the country ready to make their contribution to a government survey. Very small environmental groups mostly. With names like the Northants Badger Protection League, The Water Purity Watchdog Society - South Devon Housewives District Branch, The East Anglian Hedgerows and Ditches Conservation Consortium etc. (If my memory serves me).

A far cry from the money-earning anguish of a young Asian boy who dumped his huge basket of ironing board covers, dusters and floor mops on our porch step just before Christmas. It was 8.30 p.m., bitterly cold and pouring with rain. He was hoping I would "support him in his bid to get back into full employment." One of my neighbours, "two doors down," he said, "had just punched him on the jaw and could I see the bruise?" I couldn't, but he seemed shaky and I pictured Alf in his cups being interrupted in the middle of East Enders, so I offered the damp salesman a wee dram, which he refused. However, a piece of my chocolate fudge "made his day" and I ended up forking out £2.50 for "a magical silver polisher" that I didn't want. He told me, admiring the fairy-lit tree, that he was a recent convert to Christianity from Islam, and that his girlfriend was "giving him his first cross for Christmas."

I have to confess that I toyed, sceptically, with the possibility that all this punching and converting was part of his sales-talk. But then, yesterday, I fell into conversation with our neighbour *three* doors down. He was erecting some railings. Very high, pretentious railings, black with gold spikes at the top. I asked if he was going to be looking down his nose at us from behind them but he said they would certainly "help to keep the bloody beggars out! "

"I see. So it was you who lashed out at the harmless young Muslim with the dishmops!"

"Too right," he says, "I thought he'd have our front door in, smashing that great basket down. I said to my wife 'We're being raided!' And I'd only just painted the door!"

(And there was I suspecting the mild-natured Alf).

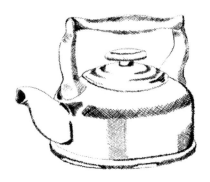

March

Getting ready for this morning's jog took a little longer than usual

Getting ready for this morning's jog took a little longer than usual. A small spider had taken up temporary residence in my left trainer. Whenever I peered in I could see him going about his business, unperturbed. No thought of trespassing. But whenever I upturned and shook the shoe, he legged it down to the toe end, possibly to collect his parachute. The fourth shake dislodged him and he was last seen disappearing into a Hush Puppy. One of his great uncles used to inhabit the bath, or possibly plug-hole. It must be very inconvenient regularly having all your furnishings washed down the drain. He had to be very carefully lifted on to a talc-coated spindly tradescantia on the windowsill whenever I wanted to borrow the bath. Later he would be seen easing his way back down the tiles and avocado enamel in the direction of the drain. When I reported this to Alastair, (believe me, with a minimum of eighty hours a week spent quietly alone together, we touch on an unusually wide range of topics,) we considered an alternative tactic of washing him gently down with a half tumblerful of lukewarm water before running the bath. My view was that, though such a course seemed compassionate in the short term, the longer term prospects for our guest, when a bathful of piping hot suds was later unleashed into his lair, were palpably less promising. The matter was resolved a day or so later by the failure of the spider to emerge from the plant at all. And, though searched for, he had apparently disintegrated into the potting compost.

Had a similar tragedy overtaken most of the Spring flowers this year? I looked out from the kitchen on the even more meagre than usual scattering of March daffodils. There were certainly not enough to do much in the way of fluttering and dancing in the breeze. But later, when I went to get out a packet of peas and glanced up at a large cardboard box on top of the freezer, I remembered where I'd put all the bulbs when I dug them up to make way for the busy lizzies. More significant events had crowded out the bulb-planting. But I did better with the pruning. I think. After my efforts with the secateurs and lopper, our apple tree is at least 50% smaller. I had threatened it with total extinction if we had another season when all it grew was mildew. I've got some insecticide by the back door ready for "the first signs of bud." So far I haven't detected any sign of anything!

I regret to report that I stood for some time, lemon-like, at the door of Boots yesterday before it dawned on me that it was not the automatic kind. I hadn't spotted that it said "Push to Open." I had to pretend I'd been waiting for someone. In Alastair's day centre newsletter this month, someone has contributed the thought that "Happiness is finding your reading glasses before you've forgotten what you wanted them for." I remember smiling smugly at the thought of such foolishness, but I'm afraid so far twice in the last fortnight I have spent up to five minutes looking for mine only to discover them hanging round my neck on the chain I invested in precisely to avoid these annoying daily searches. I did wonder last week whether in fact I needed new glasses when

I happened to glance up from my desk in the front bedroom window and notice the gardener at work in our neighbour's rockery at number 52, pulling up the weeds and throwing them shamelessly over the wall into Number 50.

What do you do when it's time to assemble "a wash"? I potter round upstairs and chuck things over the bannisters into the hall. There they are married up with Alastair's contributions from his "hospital bedroom" downstairs, in appropriate low or high temperature batches. This is more often than not the moment when a visitor knocks at the front door. This morning it was a thoroughly respectable and doubtless neat and tidy elderly spinster friend who found herself wading through knickers and bras to get to her "elevenses" in the kitchen. For a moment I feared she was going to get her heel caught in a pair of Alastair's Y-fronts. She was of course the epitome of good breeding and you would have sworn she hadn't noticed. She passed through as nonchalantly as one might through a carpet of autumn leaves. And as I disapprove of people who will say, "Please excuse the mess," I just waded through after her and put the kettle on. My next door neighbour has a notice just inside her front door: "Boring women have immaculate homes." I think I partly agree with her. But I'm honest enough to recognise that there's an element of envy in it. I would *like* to have more of an "ideal home."

May
I went to interview someone in Cowcross Street on Thursday

I went to interview someone in Cowcross Street on Thursday. A warm day in May. On the way home I remembered one of the books salvaged from Old Rob's home, "The Streets of London." My old friend Rob died a few weeks ago. He was 98 and still doing sponsored cycle rides round the London pubs for charity and still plagued by recurring nightmares about muddy death and destruction in the trenches. With his death, the Firs Estate has lost a bit of history, just when I was making progress in encouraging him to get into the car with legs tight together, like the royals, to lessen the likelihood of a trumpeting fart. He used to call me "a good scout." I got him one of those red buttons to press in an emergency but I might just as well not have wasted my time. He fell down in the snow one winter's dawn, fetching a hod of coal from the shed, and lay there for several hours till his neighbours were up and about and heard his cries. He "didn't like to bother anyone on such a chilly morning."

I've heard the last of his adventures now. He lied about his age to enlist in 1914. (Ironically enough when I ferried him to the hospital for an X-ray last year they took me to one side and asked me why he had lied about his age to *them*. "He can't have been born in 1898," they said. But they were wrong).

He told me countless sniper tales:

"I used to look through the sights into the German lines and see a lad no older than me with his head sticking up over the parapet. How could I kill him? I used to shoot just to one side."

He never got used to collecting up his friends from no-man's-land in several pieces. He came back a vegetarian after the horrors of the abattoir where he worked after he was taken prisoner. When his twenty-first birthday came round there were no school friends to invite. They were all dead.

I'll always remember his description of his arrival home from the war. I heard it many times. He'd been away for four years, survived in trenches, fallen into enemy hands, seen sights he would never be able to eradicate. He was not expected. The family had not been informed. No-one was at home. So he let himself in through the unlocked back door and fell asleep in front of the Ideal boiler in the kitchen. His sister returned from school.

"What've you done with your hair?" was her greeting.

But soon his mother would come. "I was waiting for her," he used to say, and he would hold open his arms as if still yearning for her embrace. "She came in and saw me sitting there and said, 'I expect you'd like a nice cup of tea.' "

I looked up Cowcross Street in his book. What a let-down: Someone called Stow just says "a cross once stood there," but he does not explain why it was called Cow Cross. Who was this Stow? I'd have been sorely tempted to embroider so flimsy a Stowism if I'd been the editor. Still, I noted that the River Lea, according to Professor Ekwall, was named after the Celtic divinity, Lug. I think we can all manage the Haymarket and Birdcage Walk and Gunpowder Alley. But Gutter Lane isn't at all what you might think. It was named after some Danish chap in the time of Henry III, called Goderun. The Caledonian Road sadly derives its name from the asylum established there in 1815 "for the children of Scottish parents."

There was a shoeshine boy outside Simpsons, Piccadilly last week, just along the road from the French Tourist Office. In Lisbon, one of the cities Alastair introduced me to, the shoeshine boys stick quite literally to the tried and tested spit and polish technique and any lingering in their vicinity is ill-advised. It's just as well for spiders that *they* don't need to wear shoes. With six feet it would work out expensive. I heard a programme on drug research yesterday in which spiders were used as guinea pigs, so to speak. Those on marijuana became very lazy and completed only half a web while those on speed, appropriately enough, doubled their spinning rate but then dropped dead before copulation. As a result, the reverse of a situation common in some of our inner cities pertained, in that "there was a well-advanced home-building programme, but no families to live in them."

July
Have I ever told you about our supper group?

Have I ever told you about our supper-group? A dozen friends
round the table, in each home in rotation, every few months.
Taking it in turns to provide the meal. And a guest, someone
outside the group, who's willing to provide a sort of after-dinner
liqueur in the form of a ten-minute talk: some personal
reflections, aspirations, or perhaps past adventures "recollected
in tranquillity." We've had a magistrate, a taxi driver, a
photographer, a docker; we've had parsons, shop workers,
doctors, businessmen.... I recall particularly the classics teacher
of long standing who found himself suddenly on the dole when
a new broom was appointed as headmaster and swept him out in
favour of media and business studies. When the shock wore off
he got a job as a coach driver with Wallace Arnold and was
soon being well paid to conduct holidaymakers round the great
ancient Greek and Roman landscapes and buildings which he
could scarcely have afforded to visit in the past. And what a
bonus for the tourists! A driver with encyclopaedic knowledge
of every site, combined with the exuberance of a schoolboy just
beginning the long summer break and with no intention of
going back.

It was the Whitefords' turn last night. Theirs is now the

only home in the group that we can access. We go round through the garage and across the back lawn, with the wheelchair leaving deep tramlines in the grass. But they make light of my concern. One of their neighbours was the speaker. We were spellbound. He shared with us all the details of his lifelong dream to walk the ancient pilgrim route to Santiago de Compostela. His idea, he said - once he retired from his nine to five job in a hospital lab - was simply to pick up a rucksack and walk out of the house, down the path, out of the gate in the direction of Dover. Then across France and down into Spain. He wanted to sample the open road, the countryside, the simple life. "Away from it all." It sounded enchantingly romantic. An irresistible prospect. We pictured him asleep under the stars on warm Mediterranean nights, perhaps accepting hospitality from villagers on the way, sharing a companionable glass or two of local vino with his fellow Europeans. Plenty of fruit picked from the hedgerows, eggs from friendly farmsteads. We were just about to wind up and get our coats on when one of the group enquired what his wife planned to do in his absence. Mary? Well, of course, she was going along too, to link up with him at prearranged venues each evening, with the caravanette, the mobile phone, comfy beds and a well-stocked freezer.

It's just occurred to me that some time ago I promised you some more A Level "howlers" from the 1970s on the topic of Chaucer's Canterbury pilgrims:

"Chaucer was the father of all his contemporaries.... The Wife of Bath had low standards owing to her enjoyment of promiscuousness....Her fourth husband would have liked to lock her up in a chest so as to curtail her misgivings....The Monk had abandoned the addicts of St.Augustine....The Parson was notable for his virtuosity....Indeed he was the epitaph of virtue....He would go to visit his parishioners in any circumstances, including weather....The Pardoner tricks the people by selling relics of saints who aren't....He uses extortionate exclamations....The Prioress is portrayed as a woman, which she very much should not have been.... The Shipman would throw people overboard without a thought. This indicates that Medieval people had impulsive instincts.... The effect Chaucer is trying to achieve is apparent because he succeeds.... he paints a very black, satirical picture but it does relieve the monotony which might have occurred if all the pilgrims had been devoted to God." (You can see why I couldn't throw them away).

The "Neighbourhood Watch" bulletin has just arrived. "No muggings on the Firs Estate this month." Good news indeed. I see one of the watchers up the road has been doing overtime compiling a complete dossier on the driving schools using our desirable network of tree-lined avenues as a training ground. There are more than two hundred driving schools, he reports. It's quite true that I rarely stroll to the postbox without pausing to admire the tense efforts of yet another 17 year old reversing round the corner or straining to detect the exact moment when the brake should be eased up as the clutch engages, to avoid stalling the engine for the umpteenth time. I believe there have been complaints from some residents, especially those on corner plots. Personally, I find the presence of legions of learners perfectly acceptable; after all, they reflect the fact that ours is a peaceful estate. It can't become a rat-run, because you can't go anywhere once you get in, except out again. The L-plate brigade are a sobering reminder of the days when a three-point-turn loomed before me, too, as a challenge of daunting complexity. And now that "failure to park within the marked white lines" carries a heavy penalty in your average supermarket car park, it's as well to master that particular manoeuvre from the start.

It's over a year now since Alastair's stroke. I'm called a "carer" now. But I'm still a complete beginner. Each day presents a fresh obstacle course. I doubt whether I'll ever be able to shed my L-plates. I certainly couldn't pass a test.

September
Yesterday evening I was sitting on the pavement outside the house in the rain

Yesterday evening I was sitting on the pavement outside the house in the rain with a young policeman when it occurred to me that another letter was due. Not that there is anything particularly newsworthy about the involvement of the constabulary in our lives these days. Only last week I had cause to contact them to announce the theft of my silver-grey Passat. A disconcerting and costly felony about which they will be able to do absolutely nothing. And as no homicide or even grievous bodily harm were perpetrated, and as at least one more vehicle has been illegally appropriated in Greater London every ten seconds since, I imagine my little blob of hurt is by now a deep-buried statistic in a Scotland Yard computer.

It does hurt though. One more connection with our "previous" life gone. Alastair took me over to Little Chalfont to buy that car. We went to the garage where his company car was serviced. He'd seen a nice sensible little red Triumph Dolomite he thought I'd like, but Ellie convinced him that the silver VW.Passat Saloon was "more in keeping with Mother's image." I'd never thought of myself as having an image. Anyway, Alastair bought me the car. But it's gone now and I sense I'll never see it again.

In this same week, by unkind coincidence, the insurance

on Alastair's company car has finally run out. They've been wonderfully kind in allowing me to keep it for so long. But now it must be returned. With both cars gone we would be marooned. So for the first time in my life I have had to buy a car on my own. And I have. Another Passat, an Estate car this time, blue, J Reg. And that's why I was outside sitting on the wet pavement. Once bitten, I was definitely not shy of calling out the forces of law and order to help me fit a hugely weighty bright yellow clamp to the wheel for the night so that it would still be there in the morning. Our garage will be inaccessible for as long as the builders are here. It's full of cement and aggregate and tiles and hardboard and all the other ingredients of a massive "home-conversion." (A wheelchair changes things.) So, as long as the builders are here, I'll be out there every night, grappling with padlock and key in the gutter. If you've never tried fitting a clamp to a car, I can tell you it's heavy and it's hard. At first the police station received my telephone request for help rather coolly:

"Has someone stolen your car?"

"No."

"Has someone tried to steal your car?"

"No"

"So why are you ringing us?"

"Because I'm trying to *stop* someone stealing my car."

"And what do you think *we* can do about it?"

"Well, I thought you were probably into crime prevention, and I also thought you probably had somebody there who knows how to fit a clamp on the wheel of a car and could instruct me in how to do it, and I have just put my seriously disabled husband to bed, and it's nearly midnight, and I'm a woman alone out here in the dark and the pouring rain and I need help..." (I became quite florid.) A friendly young constable drove up shortly afterwards. The poor chap had evidently drawn the short straw. He was seriously deficient in clamping expertise, but it was nice to have company while we sat on the pavement in the rain and worked it out together.

I have to remind myself that ours are the names on the deeds of Number 31. We may be the "owner-occupiers" but sometimes we seem to be in the grip of a take-over bid. Right round the clock we have company: workmen with sledgehammers and trowels and plumb lines, night carers with those rather sad, thin rubber gloves they use to avoid direct contact with their "customers", district nurses with dressings, bent on inspecting Alastair's "pressure areas". It's very much like conducting your life at Paddington Station or, on a bad day, London Zoo. The house conversion, the agency care, the nursing: all are essential. And I *am* grateful. But the first thing I do when I close my bedroom door upstairs for the night is relish the silence.

One of the building team is chain-smoking Irish Tommy. Tommy's work output when he is here is phenomenal. But this Monday he didn't turn up. He'd been at a christening the day before and needed to recover. On Tuesday he had a funeral to attend and on Wednesday he had to recover from the funeral. Today he is moving mountains of earth, high-speeding in and out along the duckboards to the skip with barrow-loads of clay from his position eight feet down a hole in the back garden "preparing the founds." Alastair used to be into high speeds. He was known in his company as the man to turn to when you wanted something done that couldn't be done. The day of the stroke ended Alastair's business career. Only the day before it happened, he was planning his next international trip to Vienna. Now he must be lifted hydraulically into a Borough of Redbridge social services bus to make the trip to his "personal development centre".

Amongst the carers we have Barbara with her scarlet boots, about twenty stones of circularity in brightly patterned tights. A face full of laughter lines. Then there's "Gym Jenny" who always arrives late straight from an energetic workout, and "Holy Agnes", who spends her night-watches reading books with names like "Definitions of Hell" and "Piety for

39

Beginners." I expected her on Thursday last, so I was marginally taken aback to open the door at 10.40 p.m. to a cheerful - I have an idea he was dancing - Rastafarian, his hair stowed beneath one of those enormous hats. He was halfway through a bag of chips and introduced himself as Gladstone, "after the Prime Minister, you know." My most recent previous direct encounter with a Rastafarian had been some years before when I had just completed some market research one evening in a high-rise area just off the Commercial Road. I found I had foolishly locked myself out of the car and was staring at it in the hopeless and helpless way that one does in such predicaments when up lopes this swarthy West Indian gentleman, with a bevy of beaming peers. In seconds he sums up the situation, disappears with a "Don't go away" into his flat and reappears with a fine wire coat hanger. Within moments my door is open and I am safely on my way.

So I made Gladstone welcome and showed him the kettle and was about to head upstairs when I thought it might be best to rouse the snoring Alastair and ensure that his first encounter with this new, colourful companion would be safely engineered in the presence of a third party, rather than over a pee bottle in the vulnerable early hours of the morning. Gladstone proved to be entirely worthy of his superior nomenclature. And who knows? Perhaps he too will see fit to enter some gracious little comment in the night-carers' file, like Abdul did last week. He wrote: "What lovely people!"

November
We have been away!

We have been away! In this letter you will savour something of the essence of a recent long weekend "holiday" - I use the term loosely - in the heart of Norfolk. This was a great adventure. I have read about wives and/or husbands facing the sudden disability of their partner who are "determined to carry on exactly as before." I entertained such aspirations a year ago. I like to think I still do. But it becomes increasingly difficult, I find, to remember very clearly what "before" was like. This weekend, at any rate, was one of my "carrying-on" ideas. Gordon and Ellie, our children, promised to converge on us later from their respective counties, but we two set off up the M11 at a steady pace in an East Anglian direction during Friday morning. (Alastair used to favour three figure speeds if ever he got the chance. Now he is uneasy at anything over 30.) We lunched in a lay-by in Suffolk. Daisy's mobile canteen furnished us with succulent bacon sandwiches and large mugs of coffee. £3 the lot. Alastair was convinced he had spotted John Prescott tucking in a few cars along, but he may have been mistaken.

The day was closing in when we finally penetrated the

leafy grounds of the 14th century moated manor house "fully adapted for those of limited or lost mobility." The drive up to the house - more of a tunnel, really - was long, and lined with over-arching trees in all their autumn glory. The impression that we were driving back in time was strengthened the following morning when I wanted to access my telephone messages at home but "digital phones hadn't reached them out in the Styx." The breakfast menu was all of a piece: prunes and/or grapefruit were on offer "subject to availability."

The proprietor was a joy. I don't know how old I was (probably about three feet tall) when it first became apparent to me that the people you turn to when you are feeling weak and vulnerable are very unlikely to be outstandingly handsome, clever, efficient and successful people. Our proprietor was ideally suited to minister a friendly welcome to his disabled guests. For one thing he had a pronounced squint. And, as far as I could detect, he only had about three teeth. But how comfortable we felt with his kindness. The potential non-availability of prunes was of little significance.

I should explain that we had inadvertently stumbled on a "Scrabble Weekend". Eighteen or so razor-sharp brains in disabled bodies were battling it out in tense crouching duos at all hours of the day and night, in the bar, the lounge, the snooker room, working their way through the preliminary rounds of the tournament, with the aim of reaching at least the quarter finals, or even better. It was a vaguely surreal scene, heightened by the presence on every shelf, ledge and mantelpiece of elaborately grotesque creations made entirely of folded paper, left over from the previous "Origami Week."

We all thought it would have been churlish of Mildred, a perfectly able-bodied spinster of 75, to steal a victory over her legless young opponent. She didn't. But she had her moment of glory at breakfast the next day when she announced in triumph,

"D'you know what? I usually go to bed at 7 when I'm at

home. I looked at my watch at midnight last night, in the middle of my match, and I could still *count*."

We were rooting for spina bifida Anthony, a former winner of Bob Monkhouse's "64,000 dollar question". Anthony had deformities on the grand scale and long dark curls, and massive rings on every finger to add to his already alarming appearance. He clattered round expertly on two crutches of differing lengths. Beside him, usually, was his pal Bill, severely crippled from birth and fiercely proud of his briefly famous friend. These two occupied the room next to mine – I had arranged for a local night-carer for Alastair - and as the tournament went on into the early hours I was regularly restored to consciousness at about 2 a.m. as they clanked along the corridor and overcame the complexities of getting through the door and preparing for bed.

"Major" Douglas was another tournament observer, like us. He was 78. He wore an immaculate double-breasted blazer, shoes shining, fresh flower in buttonhole. Elegance personified. And still making heart-breaking attempts to sustain a proud military bearing in spite of advanced Parkinson's Disease and tremulous grief at the recent loss of his wife. Other attendees held their breath as he wove his wavering way, nobly, across the lounge. He turned up extremely late for dinner on our first evening, wandering in like a shell-shocked commander back from the front line. No-one seemed surprised. Only he, on finding us all at the pudding stage. "Ah, Douglas," someone said, gently, "Didn't you notice it was getting dark?"

So, there you have it! Gather ye rosebuds while ye may!

January
There's something I need to share with you

There's something I need to share with you: I am increasingly worried that I may be losing my marbles. I spent an hour or two with a torch in the smaller cupboard under the stairs yesterday hunting for them but without success. An alternative possible theory, that it is the world and not I that is going mad, seems too alarming to entertain. And anyway, I recall with disconcerting clarity the conviction of my childhood, when all was black and white and understandable and we were wisely ignorant, that people who thought the world was going mad were generally speaking themselves losing their marbles.

Here are some of the reasons for my worry. On January 3rd I opened the front door and found a very large envelope in the porch. It was a responsible sort of envelope. I could tell that because it was green and had a sketch of some contented-looking cows on it and a message in large capital letters urging the recipient to recycle it. It was addressed to a "valued customer" from "the milkman." On the back of the envelope were various squares labelled YES or NO for you to tick or cross. In other words, bog-standard bumph with nothing in particular to distinguish it apart from the lack of silvery sections to rub away at with a coin to find out if you had been lucky and won a skateboard. I opened the envelope. Inside was a letter beginning, "Dear Customer, may I introduce you to an exciting new range of Christmas hampers."

Now, this was faintly disturbing. My first thought was that our milkman, who is getting on a bit, had suddenly discovered a pile of the envelopes underneath a crate of out of date semi-skimmed. He must – I surmised - have realised that he was supposed to have delivered them a few weeks earlier, in December, and was now, foolishly, trying to remedy the matter. I generously brushed aside thoughts of reporting him to the Milk Marketing Board, as this was the season of goodwill and it wasn't even twelfth night. But, glancing up the road, I saw that the milkman on duty, bouncing between float and front doorsteps, was all young and fresh and crisp in new green dungarees and cap. He was clearly incapable of such folly.

It was time to read the letter again: "Please help me ease your Christmas rush. This is Christmas shopping made easy. What better way to cover your grocery needs for Christmas than letting me deliver them direct to your door." I felt I should sit down. To hell with Sylvoing the cutlery! If the years were whizzing round at this rate I'd better cram in some serious living. I read on, as there didn't seem to be any serious living to hand. I found I could immediately place an order for a "Gift Hamper" at £29, or 50 weeks at 58p, or a "Deluxe Hamper" at £69, or 50 weeks at £1.38, or an "Empress" at £199 or 50 weeks at £3.98. I put a tick in the NO box. And then spent some time wondering whether I should have put a cross in the YES box. And then threw the whole lot in the bin.

It crossed my mind later that the hampers might have contained gingerbread men. I imagine you will have noticed from the national press that gingerbread men are the latest victims of political correctness. Underneath the caption "Gingerbread Persons take the Biscuit," our newspaper records that some Gateway personnel have relabelled them "Gingerbread Persons"; they have been "emasculated" for fear that they should be the cause of "supermarket sexism." Apparently the director of the National Association of Master Bakers said "the news did not bode well for the future of gingerbread men who had been around in some shape or form since the 17th century." The columnist wondered "how long Fairy Liquid would be safe on the shelves." And after reading the article I started to ask myself whether that illustrious location which Grandma Beryl chose for her most recent wedding reception, the Queen's Hotel in Eastbourne, is even now weighing up the advisability of being rechristened.

We also have the Hackney Head. Or, as she is presumably better known locally, the 'Acne Ed', who has refused to allow her pupils to see a performance of "Romeo and Juliet" on the grounds that it is "blatantly heterosexual." She apparently explained that "until books, films and the theatre reflected all forms of sexuality, she would not be involving her pupils in the heterosexual culture." Auberon Waugh had a good column on the subject in The Telegraph. He was quite sure that "even if they prepare a version of the play specially for primary schoolchildren, 'Romeo and Julian' perhaps, about the relationship between an Eton schoolboy and an Italian waiter, it will still be seen as a bore and a punishment by most red-blooded East End kids."

And then there's the matter of public transport. It's quite possible, now I come to think of it, that I lost my marbles on the Central Line last Thursday. All we sweating commuters were standing, sardine-style, for an hour on the outskirts of Leyton Station, overlooking the extensive burial ground. I was warmly clad in my new navy cashmere Christmas coat to protect against the freezing temperatures outside. At one point, on the verge of collapse, I suggested to a fellow traveller about three inches away that he might ease open the window in the intercommunicating door. But he didn't fancy "standing in a draught." And having allowed 2½ hours for my journey to Westminster, I failed to get past Stratford. The next Monday I only allowed 1½ hours and arrived ¾hour early.

So you see that my "alternative possible theory" may not be entirely baseless. Much love to you all, out there in the crazy world.

PS Do you think I should order the "deluxe" or the "Empress"?

February
Suddenly I'm accruing certificates

Suddenly I'm accruing certificates. The Stroke Association have sent me a handsome piece of cream parchment certifying that I have been nominated for one of their "Life After Stroke" awards. I've "enabled a stroke-sufferer to go on living." I've been "highly commended." I'm "a special person" and "an example to others." I'm grateful of course. But all the same I must admit I was nearer to laughing than crying when I eased it out of its impressive reinforced envelope. Neither Alastair nor I want to be "an example" to anybody! We dream of once more passing unnoticed amongst the able-bodied majority. With me looking up at him, as I have for the past thirty years, not down.

That isn't all. Only last week I earned my BBC "Computers Don't Bite" certificate in "Mouse Skills." In the long run I dare say this more down-to-earth achievement will be of greater practical relevance. Carol Vorderman kept popping up on the TV and encouraging people not to be afraid of computers. There were "free starter sessions at thousands of centres up and down the country." Especially designed for people who knew absolutely nothing about computers but who would like to know more. We had a computer. Windows, and everything, whatever that meant!

And I *was* afraid of it. So I went along to my nearest centre one day when Alastair was at his "club."

Would the college receptionist laugh or look blank when I asked for "Computers Don't Bite"? She didn't. She said,

"Go through that door, down the stairs to the basement, turn left, out of the door, across the quad, up three steps and in through the door facing you."

I walked, in due course, through "the door facing me." The room was empty except for about 100 computers on rows of desks and one man sitting in the corner.

"I've come to ask if I can make an appointment to have a free BBC Computers Don't Bite starter session. Am I in the right place?" The man looked up, looked at me, looked round the room, then raised one arm in a sweeping gesture that pre-empted his greeting: "Take your pick! " So I did. And I've never looked back.

I have rediscovered an affinity with Leyton tube station. It always used to have a nice familiar feel years ago when Auntie Audrey and Uncle Bert lived in one of those modest terraced residences backing on to the platform. This was when I was about 6 years old, and by standing on tiptoe or jumping up and down while awaiting the arrival of the train, I could just make out their coal bunker and corrugated iron-roofed lean-to, familiar appendages to all such dwellings in those days. I can't remember ever catching sight of Audrey hanging out her smalls or Bert hoeing between the vegetables. They both worked full time. All the same, their very habitat lent an aura of friendliness to the station. But they moved to South Woodford at least 50 years ago, and to Woodford after that.

Last week I found myself back on Leyton Station en route to the theatre with our friends, Keith and Val, to see the latest Tom Stoppard revival and re-installed the station as a place with some identity, rather than just as the place where you might jump out of a Hainault train before reaching Leytonstone, with a view to grabbing a seat ahead of other

Epping-bound travellers.

But, to return to our theatre trip last week: finding nowhere to park the car at an earlier stage, Keith had happened on a nice non-yellow-lined space two minutes from Leyton Underground.Thence we proceeded on foot. On the Westbound platform we found ourselves accosted by one of a "troupe" of young Irish ne'er-do-wells, the star performer in fact. He was wondering if we had any small change. He had been trying "for hours" to raise the 70p needed to buy a ticket to Stratford, (far longer than it would have taken to walk, but that seemed an unimportant detail which it would have been ungracious to mention - though, come to think of it, possibly Keith *did*.)

In the context of his way-above-average style in the con-merchant genre, 10p each seemed cheap at the price. The invitation to swell his purse was accompanied by a vigorous leaping dance right on the edge of the platform and a sequence of wonderfully good-humoured, inventive reasons as to why he had no small change of his own. It would have been good to hear his version of why he wanted to get to Stratford and how he had got on to the platform in the first place without a ticket, but unfortunately the train arrived, cutting short the entertainment: begging raised to the level of busking, and all without a hint of cringe or pathos, as though they, and not we, were providing a valuable service.

April

As I was driving southwards down Malford Grove this morning

As I was driving southwards down Malford Grove this morning, I noticed - I could hardly fail to notice - a brown tweed trilby hat of the style favoured by Uncle Bert, lying on the road in the path of northbound traffic. This naturally gave rise to a certain amount of whimsical conjecture. The hat was in good condition. Unlikely, I felt, to have flopped out of a carelessly sealed dustbin bag as it was tossed by a borough operative into the municipal refuse lorry. The hat seemed almost to have a role to play. Like the red cones or wooden planks placed outside in the road at dawn by householders reserving a space for their removal van. Or like balloons strung from the trees and gateposts to beckon guests to a children's party. And yet it had the faintly sad demeanour of one of those single gloves you sometimes see perched hopefully on a fence by a sympathetic passing pedestrian for possible later joyful reclamation. Though the lone glove has an even more profound poignancy, prompting thoughts of the likely sad fate of its now useless fellow. Most hats, on the other hand, come singly, without responsibility for a matching partner, since the percentage of two-headed people is extremely low. I did briefly consider whether this particular stray hat would suit Uncle Bert if it were to happen to be his size. But by this time I was nearing the Green Man roundabout. Nothing much green about it now, I'm afraid, during the motorway link-road construction. "Desert Man" would be a more appropriate name. So I dismissed the probably-by-now-flat hat from my mind and instead began to wonder how the recovery was proceeding of the "sick person on a train at Stratford" cited on Ceefax as the current cause of delays on the Central Line.

Now here is one of life's more irritating enigmas: even to the seasoned city commuter like myself, it is totally inexplicable that the entire tube-travelling population can be inconvenienced by "a sick person on a train" when that person could, within a matter of seconds presumably, become "a sick person on a platform," with zero disruptive potential. However, as it happened, when I reached Leytonstone Station, normal service had been resumed. So my risky optimism in setting out at all was vindicated.

I was accordingly jubilant as I stepped on to the crowded train. But only briefly: someone offered me a seat! One of those seats reserved for "the elderly, the disabled, those with luggage or those with young children." And as I didn't qualify on any of the three latter grounds, I sustained a severe emotional droop and rather unjustly resented my well-meaning benefactor. The mood passed. There is always so much to see and hear on the tube. (I must remember to share with you some of my recent research into tube travel.) A woman opposite me was wearing a mink coat and plimsolls. Next to her was a young man who spent the entire journey shuffling a rather dog-eared pack of playing cards. I entertained the possibility that he was going for a job as a croupier, but his dishevelled appearance made this unlikely.

Behind me an unseen woman confided to her friend that she had just received her vet's bill for £109 for trimming the cat's claws. Maybe I misheard. Perhaps flea treatment was included, or maybe there were eleven cats.

Soon I was minding the gap at the Bank, and resurfacing into the sunshine. The omens were good: I found 10p while crossing Cheapside. Actually it wasn't Cheapside. It was Poultry. But "crossing Poultry" sounded like something vaguely unseemly, even repugnant–like cloning sheep–so I adapted the truth. I can't think why really. I often seem to make confessions in these letters.

Here's another one. I must announce that I am a fallen woman. I thought I was strong. Able to resist the devilish lures of the advertising industry. I was proved wrong today in the chemist's. I was completely immune, of course, to the claim that Pantene Pro V would "restore the gloss and youthful looks" to my hair. And pseudo-science cut no ice: I could brush aside the latest mumbo-jumbo of the beauty trade, being wisely familiar with all their jargon. One shampoo contains "extracts of prunus dulcis," another is "specially formulated with Pro-Vitamin B5," another boasts "kera-proteins," another is "hypo-allergenic" and "nourishes the roots with Glucasil TM Complex" and "phytantriol enhancer." So I was unlikely to be moved by the claim that Pantene Pro V was "developed in international laboratories and designed to replace missing ceramide and give body through unique flexihold technology." And I spotted a mile off the ruse about having to "use this product regularly for 14 days," a clever ploy to increase sales and establish buying habits. So how was it that I finally took the bait and recalled that sincere trust-me-with-your-life voice on the telly intoning the magic words "It won't happen overnight, but it *will* happen!" Why did I fall for that? Anyway, I confess, I did. Only, when I got it home having spent much more than usual on the shampoo and conditioner, and stepped into the shower to start things happening, I suddenly began to wonder

53

if in fact it *had* been Pantene Pro V that featured in that advert after all, and whether I might just as well have stuck to dear old Boot's Own Label (Forest Fern, Frequent Use).

June

In the light of the claim made recently by the Prince of Wales

In the light of the claim made recently by the Prince of Wales that "technology is destroying the soul of the nation, moving us incontrovertibly away from spiritual awareness," I am particularly pleased to report the following sighting in George Lane last Tuesday: a middle-aged man in a cream-coloured mac over a smart suit, who had just emerged from the Fenchurch Insurance Group offices, and who was clearly not ashamed to be seen, standing in ecstasy in the light drizzle, eyes closed, nose buried hungrily in the freshly opened lilac blooms which were spilling out of The George pub car park. You felt he was making a very public statement about life's priorities, witnessing to the power of beauty and to the glory of the senses. All day he had probably salary-earned his way through cover notes, quotations, policies, actuarial statistics, limited liabilities. Now, here he was, in his mac, exposing himself to the ridicule of passers-by, immune to the smirks of plastic bag carriers weighed down with groceries from Sainsbury's. Earth-bound feet failed to realise utterly that he was savouring, fleetingly, a foretaste of Paradise. Thoughts of the weeding he had to do, the Barclaycard bill he had to pay, the broken lock on the bathroom door he had yet to mend, had receded. He floated between worlds on the perfume of flowers. Of course, on reflection, I suppose it's possible he had just read an article in The Homeopathic Quarterly recommending pollen-inhalation for the relief of piles–but that didn't occur to me till later.

My sister Mary came to stay recently. We spent most of the weekend composing the lyrics for a musical about whales for her primary school annual extravaganza. I recall that I was putting the finishing touches to an argument between two sharks, with Mary in the grip of crabs and moray eels, when the lunchtime news broadcast an announcement from North West Water about the likely imposition of a hosepipe ban. This naturally prompted us to break off briefly from our deep sea drama to discuss the responsible contributions we personally could make in the area of water conservation. Irrigating the roses with washing-up water, only pulling the chain after a "Number Two", you know the sort of thing. I'm not sure that I had ever given the same kind of serious thought that Mary's class of eight-year-olds evidently had, to the common but scandalous practice of brushing one's teeth over a running tap. Clearly there must be occasions when the deployment of a running tap may be justified. For example, when an anxious patient at the hospital is suddenly required to provide a "sample," only minutes after his final, nervous, pre-consultation pee. A running tap can be an effective auto-suggestive stimulant. And very probably the surgeon about to thrust his hands into someone's insides can be permitted a few hygienic litres, but for the tooth cleaner, the running tap must be regarded as eco-vandalism, the squandering of precious resources for purely aesthetic reasons. After all, one could avert one's fastidious eyes from the basin till the completion of the operation, and then wash all the frothy dollops of spittle away in one good economical whoosh.

In my last letter I promised you an exclusive summary of some studies I have been engaged in on the Central Line. As I feel sure I have mentioned before, tube travel provides the opportunity for much rumination and research. This is particularly the case when signal failures or suicides are in the ascendant. Over the past eighteen months, on Mile End Station, I have been exploring that familiar phenomenon known as Sod's Law. Mile End Station is where I change from the District Line to the Central Line en route home from Westminster. I can now present scientifically compiled statistics which prove what I had previously only surmised, that the first Central Line train to arrive will always be heading for Hainault via Newbury Park (i.e. the one I don't want). Occasionally, I admit, the doors of an Epping or Debden train (i.e. the one I do want), will be closing as my District Line train draws in to the platform. The only exception to the law occurs when I have parked my car at Leytonstone on the outward route, a cunning ploy which makes the final destination of the train irrelevant. Epping or Hainault, either will do. The first train can then be relied upon to be heading for Epping or Debden. What is more, on these occasions, (i.e. when I have parked my car at Leytonstone in the morning,) I often absent-mindedly await the train on my return journey at the front of the platform at Mile End, as I would if I were planning to alight at South Woodford. Thus I end up at the wrong end of Leytonstone Station, half way to Snaresbrook. If indeed I remember that that's where I parked the car and think to get off there at all!

So there you have it. A classic case of advancing years. Still, I haven't reached Harold's advanced state of eccentricity yet. (Harold is Grandma Beryl's husband.) He confided in me recently that there is one thing that gives him a real lift of the spirits every day. My mind raced through possibilities: the mew of the Eastbourne seagulls? The trim cliff-top lawns? A glimpse of Beryl's suspender? No! It was the Times Obituary column. "Most people my age are already dead!" he said, triumphantly, "but I'm still alive and kicking!"

September
I've received a suggestion

I've received a suggestion. You may recall that some months ago, Gordon and Ellie joined Alastair and me for a weekend at a specially-adapted-for-the-disabled holiday hotel in Norfolk. Over breakfast - in a brief gap between sprints out into the garden to rescue field mice from the grinning jaws of the resident cat in a touching attempt to impose notions of fair play on the bloody battle for survival being waged within yards of our cornflakes and coffee - as I was saying: over breakfast one morning, Gordon suggested that some further account of the weekend might form the basis of my next "silly letter." This immediately presented me with something of a problem. The idea that these letters should ever contain much consecutive factual information had not recently loomed large or even small in my thinking. But I woke this morning with the realisation that life as actually lived is quite as absurd as any of my recent fantasies about discarded hats or lilac-sniffers. So Gordon's nettle is not after all ungraspable. Though perhaps not on the subject of Norfolk. I don't think I can add much to Norfolk.

The bulk of my life these days is spent in making lists. These lists do not in fact ensure that what is written on them gets done. But they impart an encouraging feeling that a start has been made. Even so I am plagued by classic stress dreams along the lines of the one I had last night in which I was sprinting, shoeless and in the pitch dark, along a shingly railway track straight through the middle of a local school past rows of unopenable doors trying to get to my computer class but already half an hour late. I attribute all this, with commendable logic, I feel, to the fact that I am having to be two people. At least, that is the best way I can describe it, because that is how it feels. I'm me and quite a lot of Alastair as well. As if I am, all the time, longing to plug the gaps that the stroke gouged out of his personality, and to restore him to his old self. On the list at any one time are assorted items like: make Harvest Supper crumble, pay water bill, plant out corms, tidy the cupboard under the stairs, collect prescription, change bed linen etc. Greater urgency was imparted to this last item by a recent feature on Newsroom Southeast about a plague of bed bugs living in mattresses in cheap Earls Court hotels. At this point I stripped every bed in the house and washed everything. But I failed to spot any bugs.

One prominent memo which has been carried forward from one week's list to the next for several months, was finally deleted last week. In this case, an expedition to Drummond Street NW1. The days when we could impulsively jump in the car at dusk to dash down to Southend for a paddle in the moonlight are long gone. Outings require forethought. A number of preliminary phone calls were made, the condition of pavements and proximity of parking investigated. The necessary travel-kit (see later) was assembled. At 9.40 a.m. we set forth, wheelchair in the back, and we gingered our way Citywards. Drummond Street is to the right of Euston Road as you approach from the north–east. But you can't turn right. Advance study of the relevant pages in the London A-Z had shown that, if you did, you would be swept into an underpass and end up halfway to Bristol. Another route had to be planned, weaving through streets to the south of Euston Road in order to hit it at right angles at one of the only places where it can be crossed. We reached our destination without a single wrong turning.

But not without a single stop. Oh no! It was on a housing estate in Hackney that the first pee-stop had to be achieved. I use the word "achieved" with feeling. A tolerably quiet private side road must first, and quickly, be located. I must lever my seat back and kneel up on it in a left-facing orientation, constricted by the steering wheel, to lean over Alastair with our special screw top bottle, haul down the specially selected loose trouser to secure appropriate access and, with luck, be rewarded with a fairly immediate response. I often knock the radio button during these manoeuvres and a burst of Classic FM advertises our presence at just the moment when a low profile would be most desirable. My clumsiness is not hard to understand: I am probably concentrating on the details of the explanation to be given to any defendants of public decency who might happen to pass by and assume that we were engaged in some shamelessly exhibitionist deviancy requiring the prompt summoning of the police. On this occasion, however, everything flowed smoothly. Both going and on our return journey. But the second stop, in the Kings Cross area, would scarcely be likely to attract any attention, shamelessly exhibitionist deviancy being the norm in those parts.

By now you may be wondering what we were doing in Drummond Street. A few weeks prior to this we had ventured on another expedition to a small company operating out of a lock-up garage in Tottenham. They had helpfully directed us to Drummond Street. We were engaged in a search for a system of clamps and bars and levers which would enable Alastair to have his camera attached to his wheelchair securely at eyelevel, leaving his one good hand free to compose the picture and adjust the focus. Photography has long been one of Alastair's favourite hobbies and the house is littered with books entitled "Which Tripod?" "Exposure Made Easy" etc. It's just possible that our outing to Drummond Street may facilitate further photographic exploits. But only time will tell. The proof of the pudding....

Other events?: my first "proper" computer class, the Harvest Supper and a burglary. I am now a student at Waltham Forest College, on the "Saturday Computing" course. I have a computer-generated yellow badge, with me beaming out of it in miniature. This must be worn at all times. (I believe my badge entitles me to use the college swimming pool. I hope it's open at one of the times when I am "covered.") Our lecturer is a north-country firebrand in baggy grey flannels and a rather sweaty old shirt. A classic top grade teacher, infecting his bunch of optimistic beginners with his own passion for formats and fonts, disks and directories. He offloads (downloads?) his wisdom at high speed but manages to make complex things seem simple.

The Church Harvest Supper was predictably up to scratch. We munched our way companionably through the salmon mousse, roast pork and fruit crumble. Relaxed. At our ease. Regrettably at the same time, other evening revellers were rifling their way through our drawers and cupboards at home in quest of hidden hoards of cash. Bras and briefs were being tossed like so much confetti round the bedrooms. Even the shower cabinet and airing cupboard were investigated. But, as the nice fingerprint lady explained later, the Firs Estate tends to attract a careful class of thief: there were no fingerprints. They all wear gloves.

The shock of returning to a fully lit house with windows and doors thrown wide and possessions strewn around every room was mildly alarming, I must admit. I awaited the arrival of the redoubtable night-carer, Geoffrey, before venturing upstairs. I could tell he was seething with disappointment not to have let himself in an hour earlier in time to grab and dislocate, or worse, a pilfering arm before our return. The usual unpromising duo of detectives put in an appearance ten minutes or so later.

61

Alastair seemed to be under the impression that they had come along to have a chat about Arsenal's chances in the Cup. We got into bed about midnight. But by the next day, when Alastair hosted a visit by a volunteer from the Victim Support charity to offer counselling and cheer, we were back on an even keel emotionally and getting quite used to the mess. Their leaflet explained that "people react in different ways to burglaries: some experience burglary as an irritating inconvenience while others feel frightened and angry." I don't think I was very frightened. I was quite angry. But in the end "an irritating inconvenience" probably comes nearest to how I feel. And now that I've filled up the claim forms and tidied up, it will soon be forgotten. As Alastair remarked, philosophically and with a highly unusual show of public-spiritedness, "the burglars of this world presumably need their harvest too."

November
It was good as always to have my sister, Mary, to stay

It was good as always to have my sister, Mary, to stay for a day or two recently. Alastair recognises that she is one of my best tonics. I was as enchanted as ever by the sight of her disappearing into Walthamstow Central station at the end of her visit, with a four foot penguin under her arm and the rear end of a large felt parrot sticking out of her backpack, (charity shop finds destined to charm her class of eight year olds should the curriculum allow time for the study of wildlife in faraway places).

At that point I noticed the stationmaster stomping up and down outside the ticket office, red in the face and apparently on the verge of a heart attack. It seemed right to pause and engage him in what might turn out to be his final conversation on this earth:

"Is something the matter?"

I expected to hear news of signal failures or unreliable drivers or even leaves on the line.

"The matter! Yes, there certainly is something the

matter. This new ticket collector they've sent me - from Jamaica or somewhere. He's some kind of nutter! The sooner we get rid of him, the better! What does he think he's doing between trains? Buries himself in his ticket kiosk and reads the bleedin' Bible! That's what he does, doesn't he!"

"I see." I didn't, but withdrawal now would be difficult. "Are there other duties he should be performing between trains?"

"Course not. That's not the point, is it! "

"So what is the point then? Isn't he allowed to read?"

"Course he is. Only no-one does. And anyway, reading the bleedin' Bible. I ask yer!"

(By this time I was beginning to warm to the pious West Indian. Even if his love of the Scriptures was rendering him somewhat unsociable. He sounded like someone worth standing up for. But I didn't think it was the moment to ask the stationmaster if *he'd* read any good books lately.)

"Well, he's not doing any actual harm, is he? He's not taking a sickie or being rude to the customers." The stationmaster still hadn't stomped off. "Could even be doing himself some good!" I risked.

Rather to my surprise this didn't trigger the expected fatal event. Instead, there was a gratifying diminuendo in his huffing and puffing and he rustled up an embarrassed laugh.

"What? What? Oh, I dare say, if you're into that kind of thing." He headed off in the direction of his "Private–Staff Only" quarters. Probably had me down for a nutter too.

Mary must by this time have been well on her way to Waterloo station. Our nephew, Jeremy, and his wife, Jenny, will have experienced feelings of well-being similar to mine on seeing her emerge from the bus station in Southampton complete with her colourful menagerie at the other end of her journey. It's good to know that all is well with the family. I do even now vaguely remember the time when I was under the impression that our family was quite normal. But now I realise I was wrong and that there really is no way of judging what constitutes normality in families. But if anyone did manage to do it, we probably wouldn't qualify. One oddity is that we are all generally speaking rather pleased to see each other. I recall once giving Mary a hug at the front gate and a passing neighbour asking "Is your sister going abroad?" "No, just down to Woolworths."

On my walk to Leytonstone Station yesterday I was delighted to see a scrawled notice beside a somewhat derelict back entrance to some lock-up garages. "Bywaters skip along here." I don't need to tell you how anxiously I observed the uneven surface of the drive and with what concern I pictured Bywaters, perhaps over-breakfasted or even arthritic and in wholly unsuitable lace-up shoes and middle-aged spread, coming face to face with these challenging instructions. But I digress.

I should mention that I am writing this in a peaceful interlude between interviews, sitting on a wooden seat under a tree in a small arcade just off Holborn. Two Arabs in pinstriped suits have just sat down on the seat next to me. They asked if I minded. Naturally I said I was honoured. A parson is walking past wearing carpet slippers. Also a girl in hipsters with her navel bulging out. On the next bench a proposal scene seems to be in progress. The man has just taken up a "semi-recumbent posture" on the pavement, with his hands clasping hers and an urgent, even frantic expression on his face. Unfortunately traffic noise makes it impossible to report on the latest state of play. Her body language is less than encouraging. She may even be crying. A bit of a bush obscures my view and the presence of the Arabs precludes the possibility of moving along into a better vantage point. Another theory that occurs to me is that he is trying to coax back her self-esteem, shattered by reading yesterday's published research into the likely characteristics of people who buy pastel-coloured cars. I must admit that when I found drivers of silver cars were usually "pompous" I drew a crumb or two of belated comfort over the fact that mine had been

65

stolen. The only let-down was that the colour of my new car, blue, evidently signals "lack of imagination."

The English language must surely be the richest in the world, especially in the mouths of foreigners. I enjoyed Archbishop Tutu's recent comments on the Truth and Reconciliation Committee's investigation into the Steve Biko murder: "We're going to have the bottom line drawn under where the buck stops." Business jargon also has a resonance all of its own. Hong Kong was identified recently as suffering "minus growth in the retail sector" which presumably means to you and me that they're going downhill. I was quite pleased to see a notice last week in the window of an antique shop: "Royal Doulton figures at knock-down prices." There's a health-club in Walthamstow with a hoarding on the roof which puts a welcome cultural gloss on its grottiness. It announces: "Now is the winter of our discount tans."

Station toilets are called "facilities" nowadays. Is that delicate and refined or just daft? I noticed last week that the Ladies' "facility" on London Bridge station was to be "closed at 19.00 hours due to vandalism." I expected to find unmentionable graffiti on the cubicle walls but there were only the familiar outpourings of desire that K.P. felt unable, I suppose, to impart in any more direct way to S.B. for fear of rebuff or swaggering derision (if both were, say, twelve). It's intriguing to consider how this strange tradition developed of baring one's soul on lavatory walls at the same time as baring other parts of one's person. At least our heroine had a sense of history and recorded the date. I pictured her returning at six monthly intervals to confirm or not as the case might be, the enduring nature of her publicly proclaimed passion.

It's probably time to update you regarding Alastair's army of carers, who have, without doubt, made our home the cosmopolitan centre of East London. I am reminded of that passage in Acts 2 - the one you hope you'll never be asked to read - about the "devout men and women drawn from every nation under heaven, Parthians, Medes, Elamites, inhabitants of Mesopotamia, Judaea, Capadocia, of Pontus and Asia, of Phrygia and Pamphilia, of Egypt and the districts of Libya around Cyrene, Romans, Cretans, Arabs." To be specific, the latest recruit is a Muslim named Ahmed. He could easily be mistaken for a fashion-conscious Cotswolds farmer in his flat wool cap, Fair Isle knittcd waistcoat, tweed jacket, corduroy trousers and brogues. He is evidently topping up his wages as a quality controller for a neighbouring borough by hiring himself out through our care agency. There's no doubt about his quality, but control doesn't seem to be his strong point. Within an hour of his arrival he had broken one of my favourite coffee mugs. And any requests I make to him across a room appear to reach him via a distant satellite, like some of those odd disjointed interviews with "our correspondent in Chile, or Saigon" on the telly. Yesterday he "helpfully" emptied the dishwasher and put everything away with the result that I was discovering cutlery in the pyrex cupboard and tumblers in with the dusters. None of that matters; he possesses the only really important qualification: he always treats Alastair with deep respect.

Spin the globe a few more times to reach the remote birthplace of the Thursday afternoon dude, lanky, jet black, with a permanent smile and shoes inset with sequins. You feel he is only with you in the physical sense, but that he inhabits a happier land where the swords have already been turned into ploughshares and the custard is never lumpy. Then there's Tinyan from Ghana, bossy in floral prints, and soft-voiced Juliet from Sierra Leone. Our jovial Neapolitan fish and chip operative, Alessandro, has just been sacked. He had failed to mention in his original application to the agency that he had a number of convictions for theft. This discovery seriously undermined his suitability for work in "the care industry." Nevertheless it's true to say that, from our point of view, he has left a gap which will be difficult to fill, an act almost impossible to follow. He has materialised, on time, every morning, on his bike, at 6.45 a.m. for at least 2 years.

67

Heat, snow, fog, hail. He has never let us down. He called in this week to take his leave. But not anything else, I hasten to add. Indeed, I was convinced that his Southern Italian "code" wouldn't have allowed him to steal from us; in his eyes we had become more or less part of "the family."

January
I have suddenly realised that I can see the Millennium Dome

I have suddenly realised that I can see the Millennium Dome at Greenwich from my bedroom window. This is not a very significant piece of information but you have to start from somewhere. I was standing on the window sill with my head half out of the skylight and using binoculars to survey the distant scene when I made the dome-discovery. It occurs to me that if the roof of the dome is eventually lowered on to its supporting structure on a fine day, I could probably sell tickets to view. I could make a small charge especially if I threw in a cream tea. I enjoy making scones. I think I shall write to Mr. Mandelson to ensure that he authorises nothing without Meteorological office clearance. To miss all the fun in a fog would be unfortunate, not to say financially disadvantageous.

I must tell you about a quite unusual scene I observed in The Broadway, Woodford, back in December, on my way to the picture framer's to collect Gordon's Christmas present.

Not that it matters what I was doing or indeed where I was going–anymore than, say, a yawning captive viewer cares, months later and halfway through a lengthy holiday slides presentation, whether it was a Tuesday morning or a Wednesday afternoon when Uncle Sid and Auntie Maureen visited the leather bag maker on the island of Formabella.

"Or was it Capripua?"

"And perhaps it wasn't leather but suede."

"Or even linen."

"And actually it must have been a Thursday because, don't you remember, I brought up all those prawns we had eaten for lunch at the bistro next door, and then we called a doctor and Thursday was his day off."

Anyway, to resume, I witnessed what I can only describe as a uniquely festive scene: a queue at a post box. A quiet, British sort of queue, waiting patiently to stuff great wodges of wishes through the narrow red-framed slot. It seemed an inauspicious gateway for so much goodwill. So many greetings to grandmas and felicitations to friends.

I read a newspaper article at the weekend about a Yorkshire man with an intriguing hobby, coin collecting. Picking up money that other people had dropped. Not that this isn't something I have been doing for years, in the tradition of my father, Rodney, who daily bore home from the City the fruits of his lunchtime walks. I had not hitherto regarded my habit as a "hobby." Our Yorkshireman had developed the procedure imaginatively by keeping meticulous records of amounts and locations over many years, and had averaged £269.21 per annum. This he gave to the People's Dispensary for Sick Animals.

My approach was - *used* to be - more informal, though of similar long standing. The exciting additional dimension of an account book had an immediate appeal for me. I imagined in years to come being able to furnish revealing statistics on the most fertile districts for five-pence pieces. I think I'd keep quiet about the most noteworthy areas. Already in three days I have four entries: 5p on Tuesday outside the cake shop in George Lane, 5p on Wednesday in the Leytonstone Underground booking hall plus 10p in High Holborn and today, 1p outside Woolworths in Hainault. An average of 7p a day so far, equivalent to a modest £25.55 per annum, well short of the dedicated Yorkshireman's total. I must get out more.

I clocked up 1400 miles in my Passat over the past fortnight. My first days apart from Alastair since his stroke. Nearly three years! It's taken me a long time even to imagine that a holiday could be a holiday without him. I kept looking round for him. Having previously written these letters about virtually nothing, it's something of a challenge having so much to write about. More than ever these days I am seeing the countryside under the influence of Bill Bryson. "Rottingdean" had never before seemed a curious name. But post-Bryson, a disintegrating cleric sprang inevitably to mind. "Tarring Neville" just outside Brighton, sounded grimly Medieval, possibly an IRA stronghold. I half expected to turn the next bend and find a signpost to "Kneecapping Seamus." On my way to Altrincham, well up the M6, I passed a junction to Shugborough. I'm sure you had but I hadn't, ever heard of Shugborough. I felt ill-informed. A South of Watford ignoramus. It seemed sad that, for centuries probably, back to the time of the Domesday Book, people had been living and dying, laughing and crying, shopping and shaving in Shugborough, and I'd never even heard of the place. And now I can't find it on any of the roadmaps we have. So perhaps it doesn't exist after all. But I saw the roadsign.

It's good to have a mental picture of all your various habitats. A mental picture is indeed all I have so far of Paul and Angela's new address. But "Vine House" is sufficiently pictorial for us to imagine old brick walls, sunshine, secateurs and a complete room or outhouse given over to the tenderly complex process of turning the abundant crops into memorable vintages to lay down in the ample cellarage. Even easier to conjure up is Caroline at "The Old Granary," rising

71

early from her bale of straw in the roof, clambering down her ladder into the vast flaggedstoned kitchen to stir up the embers and set the whistling kettle on the hearth to boil. Vanessa's current address at "Edificio los Corales" in Marbella obviously demands greater effort. But, with what I take to be walls of coral and floors of marble, she is our well-placed Spanish representative. One might have wished for a more romantic venue than Maidavale Road for Alison in New Zealand. But reports from her happy pen suggest a landscape in Wellington as far removed in appearance as in mileage from its namesake in West London. After dining with Jeremy and Jenny in their "extended nook" in Southampton, I can now picture them in actuality! And of course, fresh from my recent travels, I have also penetrated "Mole House" in Woolstone, Oxfordshire, home to Richard and Hazel, the newliestweds in the family.

Woolstone is not a village you could happen upon by accident. Indeed I was flattered to learn from Richard, our nephew, that I was one of only a select few who had found it with tolerable ease (and a road map) even when looking for it. I was certainly much relieved, having arrived in total darkness and icy rain, stumbled around hunting for the key "under the flower pot by the back door" and found it under approximately the fifteenth pot, tried in vain for about ten minutes to unlock the front door, then realised correctly, as it transpired, that it might open the back door, stepped gingerly into the still pitch black kitchen in the opposite direction to a cat, and through into another room where I at last found a light switch...as I was saying, I was much relieved to glimpse a photograph of Richard and Hazel on the wall, the first real evidence that I hadn't just broken into the property of a total stranger.

March
This letter is predominantly green

This letter is predominantly green. Not green as in bilious, or green as in the first time you've held a golf club in your hand, but green as in recycled potato peelings. Our borough is going green. Today a handsome black plastic box, nice and tough, materialised on the front path. A present from Redbridge for the purpose of "kerbside recycling." The instructions as to what may be placed in the box are quite complicated. I note that paper is wanted but not cardboard. Glass bottles (washed) but not if they contained milk. And magazines but "sorry, no Yellow Pages."

That is not all: we are being encouraged to make our own compost. Recently I came face to face with three green bins on display at the library. Of various designs and sizes and at greatly reduced prices. All cheek by jowl with the books and records. My mind was filled with the prospect of muck. Barrow-loads of the stuff. Alastair would approve, I knew. He comes of a long line of vegetable growers. His father would think nothing of chatting to his potatoes and

73

runner beans decades before Prince Charles was to give such activity royal approval. And his brother, Ian, in Edinburgh, regularly grows enough tomatoes to keep the whole clan in chutney right round till the next crop. As soon as I got home from the library I placed my Barclaycard order for a "Big Bin" over the phone and now, some weeks later, it is discreetly in situ within easy reach of the back door for receipt of daily offerings from the kitchen. Yesterday I emptied a jigsaw puzzle into it. Alan Titchmarsh says you should drop in small bits of card from time to time and I can't think of a much better definition of a jigsaw than that. Anyway there were several pieces missing and the picture was almost 100% trees so that's sure to add to the goodness quotient. Mike next door sensed my new enthusiasm for compost and kindly handed over a pailful of worms from his heap. Even as I type I expect one of them is getting to grips with an edge piece.

If further proof of our green credentials were needed, I should tell you that we have recently had a water meter installed—on a trial basis. Two beefy young chaps in woolly hats turned up one frosty morning and dug a large hole outside the front gate. When I later handed steaming mugs of coffee into the hole, now more of a paddling pool, they impressed me with their resilient sang-froid when they remarked that ours was "an easy one, nothing like your neighbour's over the road." If we find our bills are much lower - which we confidently expect - we will retain the meter. If not, not.

We have some friends - wonderful friends - who turn up almost every Tuesday evening with a hot dinner for four, on a tray, and we eat together. "We have to do something!" they say. They told us last week that they had been astonished last summer when visiting ex-neighbours, now living out in Essex, that their garden was a complete desert, with not even a flower or a blade of grass to be seen. It seems they also had been metered. And now the husband is almost obsessively unable to turn on the tap. Even the suggestion of making a cup of tea causes tremors of apprehension, and as for turning the hose on the asters or giving the lawn a nice refreshing shower of an August evening, that is now in the realms of the unthinkable. Pity really, because they had such a nice show of colour at their old address in Woodford. I think it unlikely that I will be similarly affected, though I have to confess to you that I now tend to walk downstairs in the morning and empty the left over millilitres of water in my overnight glass into the front room pot plants - in rotation, of course - rather than just pouring it down the sink upstairs. But then that *is* actually the point of metering, isn't it!

Sainsbury's had Flash on special offer today. Putting it away in my cleaning materials cupboard, I noticed that my stockpile of screwed-up plastic "re-usable carrier bags" was spilling out of the cold box where they live. I tipped them on to the worktop. There were 56. I can't recall ever re-using any of them, even though you get a penny back for every one. I resolved to start working my way through the 56 bags in an ecologically correct fashion in keeping with my new recycling, composting, water-conserving image. It would be quite simple to add one more thing to the getting-ready-to-go-shopping list: Lock doors, find purse, get car out, check Alastair's pee-status, help Alastair on with coat, hat, scarf, collect sufficient carefully folded used plastic bags from cupboard etc. I must also rid myself of previous deep feelings of distaste when seeing other exemplary shoppers take out their carefully folded, crumpled carriers. I must forget that I used to find them sickeningly virtuous. I must never again think to myself, "Here comes another environmentally aware green-wellied Guardian reader." I've joined them! I am now a friend of the Earth. Perhaps I should enquire into the annual subscription to Greenpeace. Maybe on second thoughts I'll just chuck the bags away.

This letter is coming out after a somewhat shorter interval than usual because of the number of complaints received last time round. I did mention then, I believe, that I had the problem of too much to write about, for a change. Inevitably this meant that I missed a lot out. Mary complained that my two days helping out with her primary class in Clifton might never have happened. There was not one syllable about it. Gordon was a tad aggrieved on seeing the space devoted to my visit to his cousins at Mole House in Woolstone when his warm hospitality in Balham was entirely passed over. The fact that - as I pointed out to him - the space devoted to Mole House was concerned solely with my attempts to get into it, did not help. Rather the contrary. If merely trying to gain entry to one dwelling merited exposition on that scale, how much more value should be attributed to his wide-open door and eager presence jumping up and down on the pavement, ready to unload my well-travelled bags? Gordon's first floor flat does, unlikely though it seems, have at least one thing in common with Mole House. Both are listed properties. But whereas Richard and Hazel must duck to avoid brain damage when moving from room to room in their rural 17th century thatched homestead, and labour lovingly with logs in the grate on arrival home each day, and shake hay out of the toilet paper before use, Gordon can stride, or even leap, should he wish, through his high-ceilinged city domain, enjoying his Dulux colours, his masculine décor (bicycle propped discreetly in spare room,) IKEA lamps etc. with suitably man-about-town panache.

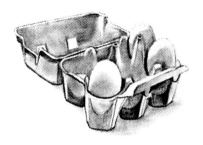

July
There can't be anything much more humiliating

There can't be anything much more humiliating than sensing that your opponent is trying to let you win at cards. Mother used to do it occasionally, when we were small, and it made us feel even smaller. I had a distinct feeling yesterday that the computer was feeling sorry for me when I kept succeeding at Solitaire but I expect it was a delusion.

Delusions probably occur more frequently with age, and sometimes these days I feel very aged. But I hasten to add that I have given Ellie an assurance that I am not currently thinking of investing in a shopping trolley. Nor do I have a regular order for specially made wide footwear, with cushioned sides to avoid rubbing the bunions. In fact on better days I still feel more than vaguely in touch with my youth. Like yesterday when I smirked with pleasure as all four girls next door, aged 3 to 12, pronounced as "cool" my cut-off-at-the-calf trousers (£2 at the Cancer Research shop, plus half an hour with scissors and sewing machine).

The world which Alastair and I inhabit is inevitably different from the one you are familiar with. I still vividly remember an experience just a few weeks after Alastair's stroke: I was cleaning one of the front windows when a family party came strolling past on their way to town for "a day out." They were lamenting amongst themselves that it wasn't as sunny as they would have liked. For my part I was still at the banging-my-head-against-the-wall stage, in deep mourning for normality. I wanted to shout out to the sun-seekers and revise their perspectives for them. I didn't though, and I try not to. As the years go by I have developed and often worn out and discarded strategies for acceptance of our strange one-day-at-a-time life together. Bulwarks against despair. New strategies replace the worn out ones. Some help out for a few hours: I think of Christopher Reeve's remark to David Frost, "I try to look upon bad days as good days in disguise." Some remain apparently inexhaustible. Amongst them *you*. Did you realise you were "a strategy"? My letters to you are lifelines.

This world of ours is a world of orange disabled-person badges where questions of "access" that never occurred to me before are of paramount importance. A request for detailed information about the widths of doorways and the presence of steps preccdes any enquiries as to menu when booking a table at a restaurant. Not to mention the availability of large loos or, as a minimum, a discreet alcove for use of the bottle. "Many a time and oft" I have held the line while waiters crawled about the floor with measuring tapes so that we could quite literally "prepare the way."

Another lurking danger which orange badge holders need to guard against is an insidious personality change. Let me explain. Special parking places, which in the old days one used to regard as a waste of the best space, are now vital for survival. Thus, those other persons who drive into them are regarded with simmering suspicion, previously not dreamt of. Especially when they leap out of their otherwise unoccupied vehicles in trainers and gym gear with a squash racket under their arm. We were backing into an "orange" parking space at Whipps Cross Hospital this week on our way to the anticoagulant clinic, when an agile young man shot into the next one, hopped out, waved his electronic key flashily at his BMW and sprinted in to the Outpatients' Department. "No orange badger he!" I thought, hackles rising. Yet he had badges propped against the windscreen in the time-honoured manner. I resolved to give him the benefit of the doubt. In spite of his BMW! "He was rushing in to collect his dear old back-bent mother. In a minute he would be seen wheeling her tenderly out and helping her into the car at his dutiful side." Then I thought, "I bet he's doing nothing of the kind." I went over to inspect the name on the badge. At that point I abandoned the investigation: the card was registered to the implausibly named Mr. Badache.

I'm sorry you've had to wait for this letter. What you have to understand - as I'm sure you do - is that the "humour" has to be upon me. In every sense of the word. And often these days, it isn't. Not that these leafy London suburbs are without their fair share of comedy. I noticed that Iceland was promoting boxes of "medium fresh eggs" last week. I expect they still are. Few could fail to relish the sight of panting red-faced joggers plainly at the point of collapse in their passionate pursuit of health in The Drive. Or the overheard conversations, or, better still, arguments, on the tube or bus, guaranteed to enliven the day tremendously.

Gentle harmless loonies are less often seen these days but we fortunately have a few in South Woodford to enrich our local community life. A gaunt, unshaven chap in a battered trilby is often on hand in George Lane, offering helpful but unsolicited advice to shoppers. The greengrocer gives him a daily mug of tea, presumably in recognition of his value as street entertainment. A woman of middle years in a floral dress and chain-smoking, occasionally invades his territory. Her speciality is political and social commentary, shouted out in awe-inspiringly filthy language for the edification of all. She generally tries to buttonhole individual pedestrians to whom she can impart her views, and the slightest sign of inattention or a wish to move on is met with a shower of expletives.

The TV truly is a source of wisdom without rival. I learnt today that 96% of all candles are bought by women. Quite how this statistic was calculated was not divulged. Is there a secret key on all tills to enter the sex of the purchaser? We were supposed to understand from all this that women are infinitely more romantic than men. It seems more likely to be proof that probably 96% of *all* household shopping is done by women.

As for romance: in the dentist's waiting room last week, (another source of small pearls of wisdom), I read an article entitled "How to Understand Men." I thought I ought to mug up on it after all these years. It explained to me that when a woman, after six months in a relationship dares to say something like "Well, we've been together for 6 months already!" and then there is silence and he makes no reply, *she* will be fraught with terror that *he* is thinking "Oh, I see. She wants to tie me down. She's got marriage in mind. Isn't that typical of women. Now I feel trapped." And she spends all the next day in tearful talk with her confidante, worried sick that she has made a mighty howler and will never see him again. But really he hadn't been listening to what she was saying at all, and what he was really thinking was "I must remember to top up the oil in the sump and clean my football boots."

I expect you are awaiting an update on my coin collection. Yesterday Leytonstone Bus Station yielded one penny. And in the grounds of the hospital I rescued a two pence piece. This, in two days, might have represented something of a surge in pavement revenues had it not been for the busker with guitar in the subway down to the tube. My contribution to his coffers left me with a net deficit of 17p for the day. I'm afraid I have fallen well short of my role model in Yorkshire (see January letter.) My total uptake for the first six months of the year was £3.53, with 5p and 10p pieces predominating. The most profitable day was June 17th, when I picked up £1.20 on a Victoria Line train near Finsbury Park. Perhaps the most intriguing was May 4th, when I discovered 5p in a cobbled street at the birthplace of William the Conqueror in Falaise, Normandy. I wanted to turn to Alastair at that moment and share the triumphantly silly find. But he was "in respite care" back home at the Winged Fellowship disabled holiday centre in Chigwell. Out of sight but never out of mind. Never out of heart.

I see that "a 41 year old shopper in Milwaukee has been charged with cutting off part of another woman's nose because she went through the 10-items-or-less checkout with more than the maximum in her trolley." Confined as we are mostly to the home, the media in all forms provide us with a daily information stream. Until recently I hadn't appreciated the rich variety of fruit to be picked in the appointments pages. Only yesterday in our paper, jobs were advertised requiring, respectively, fluent technical Bulgarian, direct catheter experience, and even "expertise in the essential conceptual design of glandless boiler circulating pumps". Take your pick! Cheerio all you wonderful people.

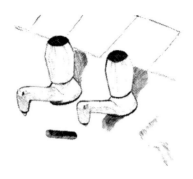

November
There have been important happenings since my last letter

There have been important happenings since my last letter: Jeremy and Jenny got married. Ellie survived a plane crash. Tasmin performed in the park. Richard and Hazel had eight puppies, etc. But, as you know, important happenings generally occur offstage in my letters. Our dramas, such as they are, centre on the daily round that hits no headlines, or even footnotes. If you have been watching Alan Bennett's "Talking Heads" you will understand that one critic asked him why his characters were all so miserable. Alan explained "I suppose joie de vivre never was my forté." It's the same with me and important happenings. I can't quite do them justice. So I stick to trivia.

I was lying fully clothed in the bath last week holding an embroidery needle. The position was an awkward one with my head at the wrong end (of the bath) looking up at the taps. Perhaps some of you have fashionable spa taps like we do. They decant the water jet into the bath through dozens of tiny holes so that it emerges in an invigorating aerated torrent, a mini Niagara. At least it does until there are only three or four holes left that are not clogged up with limescale. At this point the embroidery needle comes into its own. It's good that my embroidery needle has this secondary function, as I don't seem to be fitting in much embroidery of late. I fleetingly wondered if I was missing out in that department when a school friend I met up with after 35 years announced to me that she was "passionate about cross-stitch." We were on Roding Valley Station. It was pouring with rain and blowing a violent gale. I may have misheard her.

It was raining again this morning when a young man who reminded me of Forrest Gump knocked at the door. He had a British Gas logo on his breast pocket. I couldn't take my eyes off him: the gentle forward-leaning stance, the anxious eyes, the grateful agitation as I placed my electricity and gas files on the table before him and got on with my lunch. Not that I tasted it really. I was too busy savouring his Gumpian voice. Almost, but not quite, a stutter. Odd little nervous gaps while he formed his tongue round the next word and painstakingly delivered his well-rehearsed script. "British Gas would guarantee that their prices would undercut any local competitors. And I would have the assurance of being with a long-established reputable supplier. And did I by any chance know whether I paid by direct debit or by monthly cheque?" What a relief when he completed his list of questions. It was as if he had been daring to ask if I picked my nose in the toilet or favoured women in top positions. But what startling fluency when he suddenly stood straight up and proclaimed "My name is Vincent Kitchen," with such an exact echo of Gump's tones that I even allowed myself to wonder if he was a "resting" actor brightening up a boring gas-sales job by adopting a different persona every day.After he had gone, I even started to visualise the sales spiel à la Bogart, Conti, Hopkins, Thaw. Then I went and hung out the washing and tied up the rubbish sacks.

Don Steven, an aged saint of my acquaintance, wishes to offer the shelter of his garage to a tramp for the winter period. I say "wishes to offer" because, as I understand it, the tramp has tramped off, as tramps do. So, unless he tramps back, smartish like, or even somewhat dishevelled, the issuing of the invitation could be problematic. (This all puts me in mind of a very dear school-friend of mine whose husband, Roger, arrived home one evening from his highly-paid employment with IBM with an exceedingly malodorous tramp whom he had invited to dinner. This was just a short-stay tramp. He left the same night with all the best silver.) Those who know dear 90 year old Don are surprised that his dear 92 year old sister Marjorie, with whom he lives, has countenanced her brother's open garage door policy. One wonders in fact if any kind of planning permission might be required to change "the registered function of an outbuilding from motor to human habitation." (Perhaps some such nicety may have been in the mind of the Bethlehem innkeeper.) I'd certainly like to witness the hapless Redbridge Council employee who would stand against our Samaritan nonagenarians. There is probably a thoroughly politically correct reason why Don and Marjorie should "pass by on the other side." Or rather encourage the tramp so to do. I hate political correctness. If political correctness wins the day the whole world will be populated by persons. And where's the fun in that! The other occupants of Glengall Road have probably not been consulted about the plans, of course. One imagines they could feel led to get up a petition, particularly if the tramp in question were to establish a cheery commune of vagrant colleagues in their midst for the season of goodwill. Come to think of it, I'm a bit short of tenors and basses for the Christmas choir. Perhaps they could sing for their shelter. But I'm rambling, (appropriately enough). The whole matter is entirely academic anyway if the designated roving invitee is by now passing through Hatfield Broad Oak en route to Braintree.

To be honest, I would be very surprised if my own appearance in Sainsbury's last week didn't stir up a compassionate well of pity in the hearts of local good-doers: I realised when I got home that I had dawdled over the delicatessen and chatted at the check-out with my raincoat on inside out. I worry that this sort of thing signals the onset of irreversible decrepitude. It's amazing nobody mentioned it. Too embarrassed, probably. I expect there were a few public-spirited calls to Social Services. It wouldn't have been the label at the back of the neck that gave me away. It's quite common these days for clothing to double as promotional material for the manufacturers. But two large pocket linings flapping at either side may have created a smirkworthy bat-like appearance.

I've installed a Picasso in the bathroom. Not hung. Just propped up on the side of the bath. Not his cubist period, which could be disturbing just at a time when one is trying to relax. His pre-cubist "blue" period. Only £2.99 at Oxfam, including frame. And money well spent! A wistful, rather shadowy nude standing peacefully soaping herself in what looks like a huge shallow circular ceramic bowl on a rug in her bedroom. A rumpled bed in the background and an old armchair draped with a patterned throw. Isn't it extraordinary how what is essentially a bit of paper covered in brushstrokes can introduce a great speculative wedge of companionable life into a room. I suppose it's only the same sort of miracle as millions of tadpoles on black lines turning out to be a Beethoven symphony, or squillions of squiggles with a quill pen on parchment turning out to be "Hamlet." That's Art for you. Anyway, Picasso seems quite at home next to the Badedas. I'm back in the bathroom where I began.

January
My exhaust pipe was amputated this morning

My exhaust pipe was amputated this morning. It was barely hanging on yesterday as I emerged from Tesco's car-park in Leytonstone and thereafter the end that had broken loose bounced along the road underneath the car making a severely embarrassing din and causing passers-by to turn and stare as if I were Lady Godiva or Prince Harry on skis. I crawled carefully home at hearse pace or even hearse-with-a-learner-driver pace. I sought the face-saving privacy of the garage. There I subsequently lay on the concrete floor with a leather belt and a length of washing line, an extension lead and a table lamp. Icy rain was seeping under the door. I peered up at the underside of the car with a view to securing the pipe temporarily, pending more professional treatment by my mechanical friends at Stevens in Wanstead today. I emerged about twenty minutes later, filthy but flushed with modest pride in my elaborate securing and hoisting arrangements. I even remembered the formula for "a knot that won't undo," hammered into my head over some years by my sailing instructor and now at last proving to be truly useful. The small posse of mechanics who greeted my early arrival at the garage today gazed open-mouthed at my repair work with what may have been awe or possibly disbelief. Seconds later they hacked the whole thing off. I sat beside a rusty fan-heater out the back with "Middlemarch" while they made matters safe enough for me to drive away again. I couldn't help noticing that they didn't seem to have a toilet on the premises. But apparently they use the public convenience over the road in the park

I have become something of a connoisseur of toilets over the years. I've never had quite the same fear of French-style roadside "croucheries" as evidently grips many of my compatriots. From one French holiday to the next it's not always easy to remember exactly what the correct stance is if one is to avoid mishap. But the challenge outweighs the awkwardness, I find, though I pity those with weak calf muscles upon which success entirely depends. The toilets at our MORI offices in London all share an unusual design feature, introduced I feel sure by an architect with a unique sense of humour. He incorporated floor to ceiling mirrors. So you sit there looking at yourself looking back at yourself, keeping yourself company, so to speak, but certainly not in a position in which it would be possible to take yourself too seriously.

Going from office to grandiose office in the City I have had an above-average number of opportunities to observe and appreciate these elegant sancta and their plumbing arrangements. This has helped to build up the extensive knowledge base which I would recommend as essential for any really confident regular user. One common but quite understandable mistake I have now learned to avoid is that of failing to note which door you came in by. Naturally it can happen that you are in a hurry at the point of entry, but when it comes to locating the exit, you often find yourself confronting several identical doors with no handy arrows to guide you through. On many occasions I have found myself in a broom cupboard with vacuum cleaners and bottles of bleach and even the cleaning lady's change of underwear or the entire stock of toilet tissue for the twelve floors of personnel. And that's just the moment when a member of staff comes in and you would so like to look as if you were, say, a health and safety inspector doing a spot check on hygiene levels in the building, rather than a dim-witted visitor with an ill-developed sense of direction.

Then you need to solve the mystery of the flush. Gone are the simplicities of the good old chain-pulling days. Often it's a lever. But does it go up or down? (It sometimes comes off in your hand if you opt incorrectly.) Sometimes it's a button. But where? Sometimes you must use your foot, or even elbow. Sometimes you just close the lid. Turning on taps used to be an accessible enough skill, too. You did exactly that. You turned them on! Now you push or pull, you press a button with your toe, you ease a lever to left or right or up or down. Occasionally you just place your hands under the tap, and out comes the water. As for temperature control, that is something of a fine art. The same tap can be manipulated in all directions rather like those joysticks in the early computer games, to produce a fast or slow emission at any temperature between scalding and brass monkey cold. When it comes to getting dry, I rate those dear old-fashioned continuous towel rolls way above the press-button blasts of hot or more often cold air. Doubtless the latter are more hygienic but they take at least four times as long to do the job. If they do it completely at all. Paper towel dispensers could reasonably claim to be a convenient middle way, if they reliably dispensed paper towels. But often they are empty or, if they are full, they not infrequently dispense six surplus towels on the floor as you attempt the delicate manoeuvre of easing out the first one.

In private office blocks you're sometimes lucky and find notices up on the wall, which afford you a little intimate glimpse behind the scenes. "Don't forget it's Maud's day off on Thursday." "Contributions for Colin's retirement present to Dot by Friday please." One recent gem I took the trouble to copy down on the back of my Standard read: "After you have used the toilet, if needed, please use the air freshener and the toilet brush provided, as it is unfair on the person using the toilet after you."

Notices of all kinds can be rewarding. I paused in Sainsbury's fruit department on Monday and weighed up the worth of gaining "25 extra points when you buy two medium paw paws." I was tempted, but I'd really only gone in for bread and milk. The borough of Waltham Forest has a special gift in the field of notices. I sometimes wonder what percentage of ratepayer-income was earmarked for the production of hundreds of smart placards now attached to lamp-posts across the area to let us know that they are "working to secure London from nuclear threat." Another soothing series of council communications invites us to phone Clarence if we have any worries about street lighting or uneven pavements. Purists like me can't help sniggering a bit when passing The Jolly Sailor in Hoe Street, which advertises a "happy hour, 4-7 p.m. every weekday." My building society has a smart, professionally printed announcement at the entrance stating that

"Hours of Business are: Monday to Friday 9 a.m. to 5 p.m. Wednesday 10 a.m. to 5p.m." with no recognition apparently of the mutual incompatibility of these two statements.

It was a great relief to send off my Sunday Telegraph Enigma crossword solution today. Several times recently I have not only failed to complete the puzzle but was unable to understand the solution provided three weeks later. On such a day only a Belgian bun will do, the largest one at the front of the window with the most icing on it. Of course you then have to fast for the rest of the day. I'm not seeking to achieve the starving waif look currently de rigueur on the catwalks, but I do at least like to be able to do up my trouser buttons. I received a revelation in the garage last week regarding mushrooms. They must be the all-round perfect food for slimmers. I needed some for a recipe just after New Year and was inveigled into buying a complete box, dirt cheap, appropriately enough. This I placed in the vegetable rack after removing the required 8oz. A week later I spotted they were rather limp and shrivelled. But a week after that they had disappeared all together. Into thin air. Vanished.

Delia Smith has apparently changed the egg-buying habits of the nation now that she has taught us all how to boil them. Sales increased by 300%. And the company who make the iron pan she recommended had to employ 400 more staff overnight (or was it 40?) to cope with the unprecedented rush of orders. Such is the power of television over Mankind. Or I should say Personkind. Which reminds me I'm quite surprised that feminists somewhere haven't taken up the case of the paper tissue. Why hasn't some latter day Emily Pankhurst protested about size discrimination based on sex? How is it that manufacturers of disposables have been allowed to get away with producing generous "man-sized" tissues and second-class standard-sized tissues for women? Come to think of it I suppose the whole history of nose-blowing is shot through with rampant but unchallenged inequality. I expect someone somewhere is even now completing an application form for a massive research grant to explore this small tributary of social history.

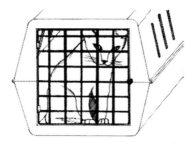

March

I was giving my salix caprea pendula its spring-time prune last Tuesday

I was giving my salix caprea pendula its spring-time prune last Tuesday when I noticed that my malus evereste and paeonia ludlowii needed more support. I attended to matters at once. I had some spare stakes from one of those "everything for 50 pence" shops. But straightaway I stopped dead in front of my lavatera albia rosa:" You will have to be transplanted," I said, "if you are not to be entirely upstaged by my hypericum hookerianum."

Activities like these loom a great deal larger in my life these days. Alastair, by his own admission, tends to get very panicky watching anything more exciting than the Lurpak advert on TV. Indoor bowls are OK and snooker is generally acceptable unless it's the Final or Jimmy White is on. Even wildlife programmes, though favoured in principle, have to be switched off if snakes appear or if adorable little lion cublets are about to be ripped to pieces by a passing hyena. One predictable effect of this inconvenient selectivity is that gardening programmes are now higher up the agenda than heretofore. We have come under the influence of Alan Titchmarsh and his like. We are into compost, propagation, fertilisers and slugicides. Life's rich pattern grows richer by the hour. Why, in the old days I scarcely ventured down the garden between October and March except to scoop up the fox poo.

We often sit in the front room window for breakfast, observing the station-bound cavalcade of 9 to 5'ers and awaiting the visits of Red, the paper boy and John the postman. Every day recently large congregations of pigeons have converged on the roof of Number 56. They avoid other roofs. The other roofs look equally hospitable to the human but evidently not to the avian eye. At first I thought they were drawn to the aroma of curry till I recalled that the Indians live two houses further down. I toyed with the idea that Number 56 had central heating in the loft and that the pigeons had cold feet. I kept a good look out - there's not a huge amount going on in Bressey Grove at 7.30.a.m.- but I never spotted anyone going up a ladder to scatter birdseed on the tiles. And though I could have missed it while milking the Shreddies, I didn't detect any showers of worms catapulted out of the chimney or croutons of Hovis tossed up from a bedroom window.

I had an easy drive down the M4 last week to Bristol to see my sister Mary. The M4 was mercifully free of deer. In fact, I've never seen a deer on the M4. Except in the designs of deer picturesquely leaping about on the signs warning you to look out for them. Deer aren't daft. My "respite break" in Bristol would have been an altogether more relaxing experience if Mary's crown hadn't kept falling off. We spent most of the time belting up and down Whiteladies Road between the school and the dentist, severely disrupting the timetables of both. The remainder of my time was passed in the school "drama wardrobe." The school caretaker was convinced that rats had taken up residence in the Cinderella section. He had been making doomful pronouncements about school closures and imminent epidemics of typhoid for several days and was keen to alert the Borough Pest Control Department so that they would have teams of hit-men on standby. I sorted and hung up costumes of every shape and colour for hours on end. Adrenaline pumped. Alas, not a whisker of vermin to be seen.

During my two days with our daughter, Ellie, in Southampton after that, I paid my first-in-a-lifetime visit to a vet's surgery. Guinness and Murphy were due for their top-up injections against cat-flu, worms, fish-breath, fleas and all the other ills that feline flesh is heir to. I was disappointed not to see Rolph Harris. But there was plenty of entertainment to be derived from the pets. And even more from their owners, trying valiantly but vainly to give the impression that they could exercise even a modicum of control over their animals. I inspected the display of specialist wares: paw-grooming kits, palatable hedgehog indigestion tablets, tortoise polish, rat talc, hamster pyjamas etc. What a relief that no-one had to face the embarrassment of using the prominently provided equipment "for hygienic disposal of accidental fouling in the waiting room."

In early May, I plan to slip off with Keith and Val for another week in France. I spotted a ten year old photo of a slimmer self the other day and thought yet again how jolly it would be to lose a stone in readiness for the holiday. Jolly to have lost it, less jolly in the losing of it. (Alastair and I spend so many hours just sitting. It's not uncommon to spend most of the evening in the loo. And believe me, after that, you're more drawn to a cup of coffee and a bun than to ten minutes' jumping up and down on the spot.) I must diet, I thought. I haven't reached the fanatical stage of blowing my nose before getting on the scales. But I haven't lost any weight either. Isn't it discouraging when you eat virtually nothing all day and wake up next morning and find you've put on a pound. I even went out jogging three mornings running (if you'll pardon the expression), at half past six, before the night carer left. Then I thought better of it and decided to settle for drinking lots of water and taking stairs two at a time wherever possible.

I was engaged in this very exercise on Wednesday, cantering down the escalator at Chancery Lane, when I caught a passing glimpse of a couple locked in a passionate embrace. Doubly transported, as you might say, by this experience. I couldn't help thinking what a godsend an escalator could be to a pair of lovers of disparate heights. It would greatly facilitate lengthy kisses without incurring stiff / stretched necks respectively. Come to think of it, they could spend pleasurable hours going up and down repeatedly, relishing the added enjoyment of the gentle vibrating movement of the machinery. Imaginative station supervisors could probably set aside certain escalators in off-peak periods and dim the lights and pipe soft music.

Still, the widespread marketing of such a scheme might backfire and result in plummeting advertising revenues. Companies could hardly be expected to waste huge wodges of publicity spend on locations where the bulk of the customers had their eyes shut. I suppose our tender pair couldn't keep them shut for too long, which might be a minus point. But at least they could take it in turns to be on watch for the step off point, given that the shorter partner would be looking towards the bottom of the escalator on the downward journey and the taller one would be facing the top going up

One colleague of mine with whom I discussed this charming conundrum pointed out that if they always used the same escalator they would soon get to know the duration of the ride and be able to time their eye-opening to the second. But such a practical solution was in my view intolerable, introducing as it did an unacceptable element of calculating good sense, quite incompatible with passionate abandonment. Then out of the blue, up steps another friend claiming to have had direct personal experience of both the problem and its (come to think of it, obvious) solution. "The escalator does it for you," he said. "When the treads start to flatten out your lips are automatically realigned!"

September
I regret to report I have just flymoed a frog

I regret to report I have just flymoed a frog. This is not something of which I am proud. As I may have mentioned, we are now regular viewers of programmes like Pet Rescue. So we have got into the habit of going weak at the knees and damp round the eyes when Pippo the ferret or Munchkin the hamster are finally found new, loving homes after traumatic experiences at the hands or possibly boots of cruel previous owners. And flymoing frogs is certainly not the sort of activity that Pet Rescue promotes! I didn't even complete the job and "put it to sleep," which is sometimes "the kindest outcome for the suffering creature," according to the screen-friendly vets. Off went *my* frog, hoppity bump, hoppity bump, into the wet undergrowth, leaving his rear leg to be composted with the grass clippings.

Talking of lethal injections, I was pleased to receive amongst the mail this week an illuminating leaflet from a national funeral society with a local branch in Walthamstow. They are developing "a new concept in death management." In fact, they say, "few people dream of how much the local undertaker can do for them." Just as well, I thought! They offer "an extensive range of coffins which you can examine at leisure just as you would in a department store." Not only that; they are "memorial consultants!" Now I don't want to tread on any toes. I certainly don't want to put my foot in it! But did you know that clients are "welcome to keep a small portion of the *cremains* in keepsake urns." Yes, "cremains". The leaflet provides illustrations of various urns, with ash capacity shown in cubic inches. There is one in the shape of a roaring elephant, presumably designed with departed "Wildlife on One" addicts in mind. It's probably jumbo-sized. Another is sculpted to look like a handful of leather-bound classics, so that Fred or Maud, as the case may be, can for ever nestle unobtrusively at peace on the living room bookshelf in the bosom of the family. One particularly reassuring detail in the environmental section of the leaflet explained the availability of cardboard coffins and "specially designed robes that conform to E.C. emission control standards." Non-smoking jackets, perhaps?

They've planted a nice bed of pansies in George Lane this week, so I was quite pleased to see some rain turning up after this spell of glittering, blue-sky dry weather. I am very grateful for municipal flower beds. It's a shame the ones in George Lane are so subject to being run over by delivery lorries trying to manoeuvre into a position within carting distance of the shop they are helping to stock. I keep meaning to write to Redbridge Council to tell them how much I value the flower beds. I've been meaning to for years. Perhaps if lots of people had written to them about the tree at the top of George Lane it wouldn't have been suddenly lopped without warning and replaced by metal fences designed to compel you to cross the road at the place where you are least likely to be killed.

Has it ever crossed your mind to wonder what road sweepers think about? Presumably, autumn provides the time of greatest job satisfaction, especially if they are paid commission on every sack over, say, 30 per day, filled. Not that I can ever remember seeing a road sweeper working at speed. It's probably quite a good sort of occupation for a philosopher or a poet. By contrast, our "refuse collectors," (gone are the days of dustmen), are always obviously in a tearing hurry. A "herald" or "outrider" appears at about 7 a.m. sprinting from house to house to pile up batches of sacks out in the road so that when the van comes along it need scarcely pause as the other team members hurl the rubbish into the yawning jaws at the back and hasten on to the next neat heap.

I called in to the ticket hall "facility" at White City tube station recently, following lunch with Gordon at the BBC. I made use of the "handmatic." I say "made use of" only in an approximate sense. I studied the procedural diagrams carefully (as in IKEA wardrobe assembly). The first image was of liquid soap being dispensed conveniently, in spray form from an unseen fragrant reservoir above the hands. This particular installation seemed not to have one of those. I fumbled around for the jet of water depicted in Diagram 2. The water shot all over my sleeves. I decided to ignore Injunction 3: "Leave hands in bowl till dry."

I don't know if "handmatic" appears in Chambers' Dictionary. Along with "launderama" and "washeteria." Even us lot with degrees in the English Language hardly know wot's wot these days. I passed a perfume ad in Soho yesterday announcing a new range of "essensuals." That was before I dropped off my negs at Kwikfoto and chose two buns from Jusbake. Of course, shopping is meant to be "an experience" these days, isn't it? I heard that every detail of the new Bluewater complex was designed "to enhance customer happiness." Right down to the last ventilator grille and rotating door. And shopping has been identified as an anti-depressant! Retail therapy! Sometimes I can't help wishing that the grocer's shop was still the place to go when you wanted to buy sugar and sultanas, and newsagents had a monopoly on the papers. You can get a mortgage from Marks and Spencer these days, and biscuits from the greengrocer and electricity from British Gas.

However, I am happy to report there *is* still the personal

touch. I popped in to William Hill's last week to place a couple of bets for Alastair. And, let's be truthful, one for me and one for Mary, who was staying for the weekend. I can never remember what to do in the betting shop so I applied, helpless-like, at the counter so the nice lady could explain it. She did. But not before giving me something of a shock: "Oh, hello, we haven't seen you since the Grand National!" (Nearly six months before!) Fancy me being *known* down at the bookie's! She was ever so pleased when I called in later for our winnings. We splashed out on pecan pie from Iceland, and opened another bottle of red.

I dreamt last night that one of our friends was standing outside the post office announcing to a small but interested crowd the identities of people who had exerted an influence for good in his life. I can't remember who the friend was or who the people were except that one was Linford Christie. So it looks as if the recent drug allegations have left his image untarnished in my mind. He doesn't seem to have shrunk in my estimation anyway! I can't say I have a very high regard for your average professional footballer. All that elbowing and tripping up and spitting and swearing. Why on earth do they get paid all that money?

The local amateur team in the village of Arcy seemed to be good all-round sorts to an homme. Keith, Val and I sat watching them one dusk on our recent holiday in Burgundy. Their modest training routines included all sorts of leaping about over the perimeter fence of the local park, and rolling around on the grass. We were waiting for our chosen restaurant to open, all three probably remembering many previous occasions when we had been four, and Alastair would as like as not have heralded the evening with a few celebratory bars of *Nessun Dorma* or *la Donna e Mobile*. We gazed at the clouds, all awash with pink and wished we were good at water-colours or perhaps oils, as one does on holiday, before getting back home to the realities of weeding, ironing, hoovering, shopping... and letter writing.

November
I must ask our greengrocer where he gets his eggs from

I must ask our greengrocer where he gets his eggs from. They are jumbo-sized. You can only just shut the box lid. I suggested to Alastair after breakfast that we might climb a mountain together before elevenses. On this particular occasion I was proposing the manufacture of a bacon and egg pie. The kind Alastair's mother used to bake. Alastair seconded the proposal and there being no other persons present, we didn't need to put the matter to a vote. I don't plan to bore you with details of the mess, the time, the effort. It wasn't quite an Everest but it certainly ran the Matterhorn close. But the emergent pie was in the end superb. What I did want to tell you about was the eggs. Only even now I'm wondering whether it's worth telling you about them because you aren't going to believe me.

The recipe required four eggs. I broke each one into a

separate small dish so that Alastair could launch them gently out on top of the smoked back rashers already reposing in the pastry base. (Alastair used to think nothing of dashing off a elaborate boeuf bourguignon or a pot of minestrone soup.) His next task was to prick the yolks to spread the "yellow" evenly throughout the pie. The first egg had two yolks. Look, I'm not going to spin this out: all four eggs had double yolks. We ended up with eight yolks in our pie. I know I should have taken a photograph, but believe me, it wasn't the moment. Getting the pie lid on, clearing up and pouring a coffee each took precedence over recording the ovate phenomenon for posterity.

But later on, when Alastair was indulging in a recuperative snooze, I couldn't help wondering if the greengrocer's cockerel was on a course of fertility treatment. You know, the sort that often leads to multiple births. I suppose such a conjecture marks me out as a 21st century housewife. I pictured your average African tribeswoman in, say, 1836, rushing out of her mud hut with the eggs jostling around in a clay bowl, in quest of the local witch-doctor to check out whether they signified a blessing or a curse. The entire village population would have assembled in a communal clearing to inspect these freaks of nature. The cook might perhaps have notched up considerable forest cred and be thereafter consulted by other respectful wives when any domestic problems arose.

I have a nasty suspicion that our own forebears in, say, 1302, would have recoiled in horror from the pie-maker and dispatched her into eternity without delay on a ducking stool or a bonfire. Not for them the civilised curiosity of the ancient Greeks who would have applauded the wisdom of a busy mother in, say, 582 BC, as she dropped her rolling pin, grabbed the eggs, called out her chariot driver and headed off at top speed to Delphi. There the priestess would emerge from her cleft in the rock through a cloud of intoxicating vapours and enter into a self-induced trance before delivering her divinely inspired oracular judgement as to the significance of this startling omen.

I know all this because I refreshed my memory by looking up Delphi in the encyclopaedia. Needless to say I am now also up to speed on Delhi, Demeter, Demosthenes, democracy and Delius. I hadn't realised that Delius was born in Bradford. His parents wanted him to go into business but he was dead set on a career in music. When he was twenty they sent him to Florida to grow oranges but he spent all his time playing the violin and hunting crocodiles, so the plantation failed to thrive.

Did you know Demosthenes was the greatest of the Greek orators? His father died when he was seven and his three guardians squandered all his trust money. It was in the process of fighting them through the courts for compensation when he was eighteen that he developed a passion for legal argument and speech-making. And this he continued to exercise all his life in spite of a serious speech impediment which he sought to overcome by practising endlessly with his mouth full of pebbles!

I sometimes think "Grape-Nuts" are a bit like pebbles. I'm very fond of them but you have to watch out for your teeth. We bought a packet on Friday. There are fashions in breakfast cereal packaging, aren't there. Do you recall we were subjected to quite a lengthy "educational" phase a year or two ago? You were very unlikely then to dish up a helping of Crunchy Nut Cornflakes without having to broaden your mind on such subjects as the invention of the wheel, the charge of the Light Brigade, the nature of the atmosphere on Mars or the daily diet of dinosaurs. There's been a swing in recent months towards tattoo transfers, plastic European soccer stars, Stuart Little bean bags and Pokémon action cards, all presumably designed to attract junior shoppers. Even Action Man is enjoying something of a revival. It's not hard to guess that somewhere in the advertising firms of the metropolis there are smiling cynics in charge of the Kelloggs or perhaps the Weetabix contract who are exercising their minds day and night with a view to setting off tantrums in young children to embarrass their mothers into buying the cereal of *their* choice.

When I located the Grape-Nuts I found there was a different trend of blurb amongst the mueslis and "bran-rich, high-fibre" varieties. Here everything was health with a capital H. There were special offers on electric toothbrushes, tennis sets, lycra outfits and snorkling masks, and columns of earnest information about the value of thiamin and riboflavin, folic acid and bone-building vitamins, and vital ingredients to cleanse your blood and activate (gently of course) your sluggish bowels.

I see that Feng Shui principles are becoming very fashionable in the area of décor. I wouldn't like you to miss two important pieces of advice I picked up from a TV programme this week, namely that the end of the bed, every bed presumably, should point to the south east and, even more vital, the toilet lid should be firmly closed at all times, except presumably when in use, "so that your good luck doesn't disappear down the pan." I couldn't help remembering a story that made the local headlines years ago about a flat-dweller in Wanstead who was going to sit down on the toilet and just in time spotted an adder in the pan. It had found its way up through the air-conditioning system, presumably from the extensive gardens below. Luck can travel in either direction, it seems.

January
The invitation on the pot said, "Please Test."

The invitation on the pot said, "Please Test." So I applied a generous daub of age-defying vitamin-enriched anti-wrinkle cream. In Boots. I spend a measurable amount of time these days waiting about there while Alastair's prescriptions are dispensed. (Since the stroke, Alastair has never experienced a day without pain. It's to do with where the blood clot lodged in his brain that day, in the car outside the house. He has "guinea-pigged" numerous drugs under the care of wonderful caring consultants at St.Thomas's. But nothing takes the pain away). Testing the "beauty products" is one way of pleasantly and profitably passing the time in Boots once all the 3 for the price of 2s have been checked out. I see that blank videotapes are on special offer in packs of 6. They carry a "lifetime guarantee." Customers just popping in and out for Pampers or denture cleaner could well be impressed by such a claim. But for the hanger-about like me there is time to wonder "Whose lifetime?" The lifetime of the purchaser? A rash, almost Blairian promise if the purchaser is, say, 8. But if not, then it must refer to the lifetime of the videotape. So what are we saying here? Presumably, that the tape will go on working for as long as it goes on working. Wow!

How are you making out with your New Year's resolutions? Have you broken most of them by now? That's what they're for really, isn't it? Rather like temptations: however regularly one expresses the desire not to be led into them one feels pretty let down if nobody bothers to try. My resolution to write to you more regularly reared its head quite forcefully within days of the decorations being taken down. If I don't get a move on, February will be looking me accusingly in the face. And if your doormat is like ours you are probably already wondering if anything other than an urgent plea to take out a loan will ever drop on it again. Our postman describes an envelope with a stamp on as "a rarity" these days. He cheerfuls his way in to the front room table every morning and has a friendly word with Alastair over his Shreddies. "Proper mail for you this morning!" he announces in triumph, placing the envelopes on the table and prodding the stamp with a gleeful forefinger. Then he completes his kindly routine by stepping across to the bureau and passing Alastair the letter opener, sometimes even pausing long enough to hold an envelope down so Alastair can split it open with his good hand. Then he disappears down the path again throwing a few meteorological observations back over his shoulder as he goes: "Nice digging weather," or "Sun hats essential today!" But, given that he's an outdoor, vigorous sort of bloke, his assessments have to be adjusted for ordinary mortals: days when parked cars are covered in frost, inch-thick, are "a mite brisk" in his parlance. Soon afterwards, Red, the paper boy, glooms in with a perpetual look of someone about to succumb to flu, or even pneumonia. He deposits the day's news in front of his customer, then retreats with a cry of "See yer layter!" which we soon learnt to interpret as "See yer termorra!"

The district nurse is sometimes the next to call. With all the delicacy we associate with the medical profession, she generally announces, "I've come to look at your bottom."

Royal Mail turned up trumps during the second week of

January: a glossy leaflet (i.e. not proper mail) arrived and announced: "In less than 3 months you'll make history." I sat down and read on. "For you, together with your family and friends, will be part of an event that happens so seldom it is never experienced in most lifetimes - the dawning of a new Millennium. How will you mark the occasion? With a festive celebration?" Here indeed was a document to cheer the heart on a chilly morning. Of course I normally expect to receive Mary's Christmas card some time in early January. And my pal Jenny is endearingly reliable in that respect too. Her greetings always materialise on the tardy side. But here was our Great British postal service, ten days behind schedule, delivering their own mailings with splendidly shameless panache and announcing the forthcoming Millennium dawn long after the entire world had finished celebrating its arrival.

On that same day the newspaper yielded what can only be described as a bumper crop of news stories. I suppose we should draw a veil (or shroud) over the account of the tragic widower who spent 3 months constructing and testing a DIY guillotine in his stairwell before dispatching himself in this revolutionary way to join his beloved in Elysium. But surely, on a lighter note (and in view of my in-depth study of the topic in a recent letter) we ought to mention the widow who "gave her husband an unusual send-off when she arranged for his ashes to be incorporated into three firework rockets and launched near their home in Cheshire. Her husband's last wish, she said, was to be scattered in the air. He certainly went out with a bang!"

There were no less than two Eastbourne stories: "a voracious army of limpets is eating away the foundations of Beachy Head at the rate of 0.6 millimetres a year." A resourceful professor and his young female colleague have been telling an environmental conference in Brighton that they "spent 3 years measuring the amount of chalk in the waste excreted by the common *patella vulgata* found on the shore platforms that extend from the base of many chalk sea cliffs." A likely story if ever I heard one. And Eastbourne General have just issued a statement regarding the temporary morgues required by the flu epidemic. Sixty bodies have been kept in an articulated lorry parked in the hospital grounds. "This was always part of our long-term planning," said a spokesman. "We expected to be extra busy over the holiday period."

We read too of the 54 year old grandma having triplets, the pronouncement in Nigeria that women's football is "un-Islamic," and the resignation of Hogen Fukunaga as leader of the Japanese HoNo Hana Sanpogyo cult, who predict their followers' fortunes from the soles of their feet. Perhaps the pick of the foreign news featured the Romanian farmer who had already killed 10 of his 100 pigs, believing them to be suffering from a highly contagious disease, before a vet arrived and told him they were just drunk. They had fallen into an alcoholic coma after eating the waste from a local distillery.

The army of carers who march through our home day by day continue to bring flavours of many distant parts of the world with them which possibly helps to counteract the sad fact that we are most unlikely ever again to taste them ourselves together at first hand! I did have a flying visit to Glasgow before Christmas. The descent on a windy December day was so bumpy I several times thought we had already landed and was puzzled to see that the houses still looked terribly small. Glasgow was its usual glorious self. There seemed to be fewer rip-roaringly drunk citizens reeling about the streets before noon than I remember from way-back visits with Alastair, though we did, one morning, come across a chap humming contentedly to himself while standing in the middle of a busy road holding up a large kitchen sink.

Ellie's two cats seem to have adopted the other inhabitants of her apartment block at Blackfriars Court and laugh behind their paws at any inhabitants who thought *they* had adopted *them*. It has come to the point now where Ellie's outlay on Whiskas need be only minimal, as Guinness and Murphy will be well-filled on tuna, salmon and left-over titbits of roast chicken from countless other flats before she returns from her riverside office to re-assume technical responsibility for the flirtatious felines. Meanwhile down here in London, Phoebe, next door's cat, spends hours daily sitting quietly staring at the cat flap we installed for Guinness and Murphy's prolonged holiday here last summer when Ellie was in the throes of moving from Southampton to Glasgow. I suppose poor Phoebe thinks at any moment they'll be out to play.

I don't relish round-robin letters myself, with their rather non-individual flavour. Some people (especially Americans, let's be fair) write of the huge successes of every member of their family in every project they undertake. I, on the other hand, often feel I'm missing the target in this "carer" role. I'm not sure what my target is on any given day. I long for Alastair to experience occasional times of contentment, even happiness, but have to settle for achieving at least some phases of relative equilibrium. I long still to be more wife than carer, but when you are strapping your husband into a hoist to raise him up into his bed each night, or easing his once powerful, now paralysed, arm into the sleeve of his jacket, it isn't easy. I long to get into his mind, to understand what our life together looks like from where he is now. But in so far as that is possible, I can't escape the conviction that I must, inevitably, appear to him to be the very personification of his dependency. I went to visit a dear, wise, 92 year old friend in hospital yesterday and asked for his guidance. "Hang on, dear, that's all you *can* do!"

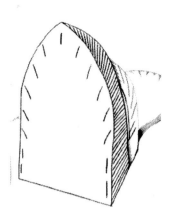

March

There was the usual traffic congestion today in Woodford Green

There was the usual traffic congestion today in Woodford Green (still known sentimentally but unrealistically by long-established residents as "the village.") At 2 mph the mind is apt to wander. Mine wandered down to the fire station, a striking architectural feature for as long as I can remember, with its tall tower at the top of Snakes Lane. Why *do* firemen slide down poles? They rebuilt that fire station completely only a few years ago and up went a nice new tower. It's almost as if fire stations have to have towers so firemen can slide down poles. I wonder if they slide down poles in other EEC countries. Even in Trumpton, Hugh, Pugh, Barney McGrew and Co all appeared down a pole. Why can't firemen be quartered on the ground floor ready for a quick getaway on the fire engine? After all, the other emergency services don't insist on poles, do they? Have you ever heard of police zooming down poles to get to the scene of the crime, or ambulance men to attend a life or death accident? I can only conclude (though I must be missing the point) that firemen like sliding down poles. It's one of the perks of their job. Perhaps if they didn't have poles there might be a downturn in recruitment figures: a short fall, you might say.

I've never had any desire to be a fire-fighter, though it might be fun directing one of those high pressure hoses. The shower-head fell off when I was in mid-shampoo yesterday and instead of being swathed in invigorating spray I found myself pelted with a continuous solid jet. I fully expected to discover holes in my scalp once I had ducked out of the stream and groped for the off switch. The whole experience has caused me to review my previously held opinion that the use of water cannon for crowd dispersal is a bit of a soft option.

The mention of soft options for some reason reminds me of another good friend, Ed. I gather he is doing some practical work in the area of psychiatry. He's managed to arrange a six week attachment to a hospital in the Bahamas. So it's obvious *he's* not losing his grip! I happened on a three inch thick tome entitled, "An Introduction to Psychiatry", when browsing in Dillons on Wednesday. If that's just "the introduction" I would caution you all, except possibly Ed, against dipping in to such publications. Even a cursory glance at a few pages was sufficient to induce anxious self-analysis. Did buttoning a shirt from the bottom up indicate incipient agoraphobia? Could a well-trained specialist read, as if from an open book, the entire history of your sex-life by looking in your garden shed and inspecting the relative positions of your spade and fork on their hooks on the wall? The book didn't appear to carry a government health warning. My advice is to stick to nice unperturbing volumes like Delia Smith's "One hundred things to do with a chicken."

Doctoring has always struck me as a profession demanding a degree of restraint and sobriety. At least in the UK. Today's junk mail brought "astonishing", news of "the best-selling health book in America." There's something delicious and irresistible about the U.S.'s shameless love of hyperbole. This "absolutely amazing book" had already sold "well over 10 million copies." You could discover "life-changing medical secrets," including the use of wet tea-bags for mouth ulcers, baking soda for athlete's foot, salt water for nasal drip. You would learn how to eliminate hangovers, achieve inner peace, clear bloodshot eyes. You would learn why you should never eat breakfast on an aeroplane, and how to cure earache with a hairdryer, make warts fall off with castor oil, and wrinkle-proof your skin. And questions you had so frequently asked would be answered, like "Does the cranberry juice treatment really work in cases of bladder infection?" Wonderful!

"Hyperbole" is in itself a rather satisfying word. It rolls off the tongue. More interesting than "exaggeration." There was a time when I could reel off a whole list of figures of speech and give examples. They always appealed to me. "Litotes" for instance: St.Paul got out of an illegal beating when he uttered the famous litotes: "I am a citizen of no mean city!" And "onomatopoeia" where the word sounds like the thing it means. And "metaphor" and "simile" and "personification" and "antithesis." That's a rhetorical device setting two ideas in contrast. There's a good example in the wedding service: "for richer, for poorer; in sickness and in health; for better, for worse." Alastair and I could not have foreseen that our "for worse" would occur so suddenly. We didn't even have overnight to prepare for it. It just happened in a moment outside the front gate on that day in May. How could we ever have guessed what that comma between the two phrases would mean in our particular case? For better, for worse. A life-changing comma!

I have a particular fondness for euphemisms. "May I make use of the smallest room?" for example. Which I think is at least a step in a more realistic direction than "I need to powder my nose." There is probably less nose-powdering these days than there used to be. "Percy has been called home" was once a popular saying, supplanting "gone to

110

glory," when a trend towards less confident afterlife expectations began to bite. Perhaps today's euphemisms also reflect changing social mores: Clinton admitted that, for an American president, his behaviour might have been deemed "inappropriate." Hamilton confessed to being "economical with the truth." School reports have always been a fertile source: "Craig can be relied upon for lively contributions in class." (He never shuts up.) "For a child of his age, Lee has a well-developed capacity for independent thought." (A precocious, opinionated, unco-operative brat.) Job references are even more fruitful:" The departure of Bill Smitherstone will be felt throughout the company." (Everyone will sigh with relief.) "I have no hesitation in saying that Glen Patterson will contribute fully in any role." (He's an interfering know-all.) One very recent example crops up frequently at 9 p.m. on the telly when a solemn voice warns of "adult" material in the upcoming film. It won't be long before applicants to enrol for "adult evening classes" are going to be disappointed when they find it's conversational Spanish or dried flower arranging.

This reminds me of some joyous hours I spent recently combing through seaside brochures for Ellie and producing hundreds of computerised labels for the distribution of Waverley Paddle Steamer timetables to potential customers. The tedium was more than offset by a rediscovery of the wonderful, quintessentially British world of the seaside boarding house. I noticed that one modestly priced family hotel was unsuspectingly offering an "adult games area." I imagine they may be facing a number of complaints under the Trades Descriptions Act. American overkill had sneaked in to some of the big chains - "Quite simply the finest hotel on the Hampshire coast" – but the tone of most of the intimate little blurbs was touching, even timid: "Past customers' comments have led us to believe that everyone who visits here will be more than satisfied with the comfort, cleanliness and service received." One of my favourites:

"You will not be appreciably more comfortable nor made any more welcome than if you stay at the East Cliff Cottage Hotel." Who wouldn't experience a lump in the throat on reading: "Ideally situated in a quiet cul-de-sac. Level walk to shops. Weekly senior citizens' discount [off peak]. Stamp appreciated for brochure." Or what about: "Full fire certificate. Storage space for bicycles. Hostess trays replenished daily. Use of iron." No wonder seaside boarding houses have been a favourite setting for theatrical farce!

Some of the copy drifted into fantasy, especially where gardens were concerned: "nestling into exotic south-facing sylvan setting," "enchanting shrubberies backed by dappled woodland." As you might expect, food loomed large: "You will be served at separate tables by friendly staff." (With any luck and careful chair-positioning you might be able to avoid speaking to any other guest.) Frankly, I was more drawn to the outrageous "superb variety of mouth-watering menus" than to "cleanliness and plentiful, carefully prepared meals." I quailed at the idea of "candlelit dinners personally supervised by the owner at all times."

Alastair and I live in a kind of parallel world alongside the able-bodied one. These seaside brochures had transported me into another parallel world, reminiscent of something out of Mr Pooter's diary: "all rooms have thermostatically controlled radiators; shoe-cleaning facilities available on request; vanity units in standard rooms; fully automated 24 hour hot water." Who could ever doubt that Britain is Great!

Apologies to those who spotted it themselves. I simply had to draw your attention to the research recently published by Chris Kettle of the University of Sunderland. He has discovered "the first centipede with an even number of pairs of legs." Despite a century of studying the world's 3,000 species, until now, scientists had only ever found centipedes with an odd number of leg pairs, varying from 51 to 191. Mr.Kettle said: "I never expected to make a find as exciting as this!" He has reported it to a meeting of international experts in Poland and the centipede is currently being examined in Italy. Professor Arthur Wallace of the University of Sunderland Ecology Centre said: "This really is a marvellous discovery which adds a great deal to our knowledge of centipedes."

That reminds me: I am knitting Alastair some leg warmers.

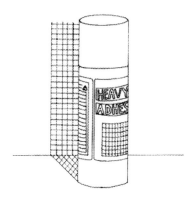

May

Last Saturday I ordered four canisters of spray glue

Last Saturday I ordered four canisters of spray glue and a medium-sized Pritt stick. From a national mail-order office-supplies company. The Pritt stick was added in to bring the cost up to £30. At this point the postage would be free. So by paying for the Pritt stick I would in fact not be paying for it, or something like that. Already I sense that you are thinking, "How can anyone expect us even to feign, graciously, any interest in glue?" I agree. It would admittedly be wonderful to begin, "Last week I booked our flight to Sydney," or, "Last week we went for a ride on the Orient Express," or even, best of all, "We strolled down the road together to buy some Velcro at Woolworths." But I can't. So let's get back to the glue. I won't bore you with why I wanted the glue. It's quite simply the most satisfying glue I know. Strictly for sticking, you understand! And with spray glue, if you get the picture mounted at slightly the wrong angle, you can peel it off again and replace it at the right angle. And there's no mess, and no lumpy bits under the surface and - of particular importance - no smell of fish!

The canisters were promised for Tuesday. On Wednesday, when I rang, they said the driver could not find Bressey Grove. We're not talking here about an apprentice Pizza Hut delivery boy on his second day. We're talking about a national "we keep your promises" type of company. "In which part of Greater London was Bressey Grove?" (They already had the postcode!) The order would be "delivered later." On Thursday "there had been some trouble over my location." I asked, "Had they tried the A-Z, in which Bressey Grove had featured since its first edition in the days of Noah?" They would "look into it." An hour or so later the distribution company rang to ask me to spell "Bressey." No glue arrived.

Now I should say this: I would be the most amenable of persons if, for example, there had been a military coup in the country sourcing the glue, or if the London water table had risen six feet and flooded the warehouse, or even if the van driver had crashed into a Belisha beacon while rushing to visit his dying mother. But to be required to swallow the surreal notion that locating a nice wide suburban street just off the A11 in outer London was somehow equivalent to tracking down the source of the Nile: this was too much.

Yesterday, Friday, I phoned early. The glue would be "with me shortly." How could they guarantee that? They had promised it for the previous day and it wasn't here! Today there would be "no problem." At 4 p.m. I was told that "the glue was back at the depot and would arrive next Tuesday." Clearly the time had come for the final onslaught. I know I don't need to point out to you old-young friends, (especially to our friends Paul and Angela after their recent long-running wedding list intifada with Debenhams,) that the key to any irate customer telephone routine is to seem to be on the point of suicide or insanity while remaining inwardly millpond placid. You need to be able to tremble and crack vocally and intermittently burst into tears while calmly inserting the next piece in your jigsaw puzzle. The glue arrived this morning, wrapped in lots of bubble wrap and with a printed card attached telling me how much my business was appreciated and reminding me that their aim was to provide all their customers with "a perfect shopping experience."

Have I mentioned lately what a good service we receive at Boots Pharmacy? The pharmacists take alternate days. So it's Babita Patel on Monday, Wednesday and Friday and on Tuesday, Thursday and Saturday you are served by Julius Ogewole Adasonla. Exotic-sounding! But even more exotic-looking! I told him only the other day he was in the wrong job, sending his customers' temperatures up when they already had a sore throat or constipation. He smiled happily in his Saville Row suit, and mentioned that if I had a Boots Loyalty Card I could get points on my hair-colourant and dental floss.

Years ago, when I used to set out each morning with my father, Rodney, to catch the Green Line coach to Stratford (he continued on to Aldgate,) we passed the time companionably playing a sort of sophisticated "I Spy." It wasn't a competitive game. We had a system of points and bonuses which could be notched up. But only under certain circumstances. For example, a lady whom we christened "the mandarine" had a points value of 5. But only, of course, if she was sporting her "mandarine's hat," a kind of inverted wok reminiscent of pictures of workers in paddy fields in the illustrated Arthur Mee's Children's Encyclopaedia. We could record a bonus of 5 points if she launched into a discussion of her health - which she often did - with one of her fellow passengers. There was a tantalising element of luck with regard to these bonus points, since we boarded the bus ahead of her, and if she didn't sit somewhere within earshot we had no chance. She could have been divulging every detail of her recent hernia op or the application technique for her medication for cystitis. But we would be none the wiser if we couldn't hear. It would have been contrary to the spirit of our game, slightly contemptible even, to move to a nearer seat simply to increase that day's score. Even more tenuous were the points awarded for a sighting of the "phantom dog-walker." A particular junction on our route represented, evidently, the furthest extent of the daily walk of a bowler-hatted gent and his terrier. If the coach failed to pass at just the time when they hove momentarily into sight before turning round and heading back, nil points! And my surreptitious craning round for a glimpse through the back window of the bus was regarded by Rodney as marginally unethical.

Alastair and I have recently developed a similar morning pastime, though the hours of amusement it took to construct our framework of eligible personnel, and to reach agreement on each potential bonus will probably prove to be the most entertaining part of the exercise as Alastair often drops off for a few minutes just when "the bouncing Hindu" or "Mata Hari on her mobile" pass the gate. We have a time-window: 7 30. to 9 00.a.m. That's when we are usually sitting in the front room, viewing the cavalcade of city commuters, paperboys, postmen, milkmen, shoppers etc.

Because so many of the passers-by are predictable regulars, there have to be extra conditions covering point-scoring to add to the excitement of the chase. For example, Sid must be wearing his yellow knitted hat. And if he waves that's worth 5 bonus points. Phyllis must be in her white candlewick when she darts out for her Telegraph in the porch. It's no good if she's dressed. Kevin must be running. David must suddenly remember something he's forgotten - a frequent occurrence! - and hurry back to get it. "Gert and Daisy" must have their shopping trolleys. The dog-walking "monk" is pointsworthy just for walking his dog and being a monk. (He has a sort of tonsure haircut.) And that goes for

Mr. Charisma too. His very appearance is sufficient to score. Mr. Charisma works in the Post Office. His expression never changes, whether walking or working, nor does he ever, as far as I can tell, blink. When he serves you it's quite hard to tell if he's awake, or indeed, alive. I must admit I have quite a soft spot for him. He dares to be different.

One morning I shocked him by running out of the house and asking if he would be so kind as to lodge a prescription request form at the surgery next to the post office. He seemed mildly surprised that I knew he worked at the post office even though he has handed stamps, airmail labels, tax discs, etc. to me on a regular basis for at least the last ten years. He received the envelope without comment and I collected the drugs the next day. The encounter has never been alluded to since, or acknowledged by the slightest twitch of an eyebrow when I have found myself at his counter to post a parcel. But I don't forget.

On one recent visit to the Post Office I collected my "freedom pass"! It's a sort of bitter-sweet occasion, granting you free travel throughout London with one hand and reminding you of your senior citizenship on the other. I couldn't help remarking that the P.O. Public Relations training is somewhat haphazard: when I went in ahead of my birthday to ask about the procedure for getting a pass, the "lady" who served me said, " 'ave you 'ad one before?" I was mortified. When I went back the following week with my photos and form all filled up, the *gentleman* who served me said, "Who's this for then, yer Mum?"

Considering my senior citizenship, I am in pretty good shape I suppose, although I've noticed recently that sometimes when I take my watch off I get a touch of cramp in my left foot. And I did pop down for a spell on the osteopath's couch last week to see if she could shed light on my stiff neck. I can still wield my pruning hook and my petunias are all planted out in their terracotta pots. As usual, the moment I walked indoors on completion of the task the word went out to the entire snail

118

and slug community for miles around: "Behold, the table is spread before you. Come in and feast." It seems a crying shame that we can't *both* enjoy the petunias. But the fact is we can't. Or *they* can't, to be more accurate.

July

I see someone has bought Mrs.Thatcher's old handbag

I see someone has bought Mrs.Thatcher's old handbag for £100,000. Old handbags are particularly unattractive items. I say this with some authority as an experienced frequenter of charity shops. To be frank, new handbags don't excite me either, but old ones, previously owned by someone else, are peculiarly repellent. Second hand dresses, blouses, skirts etc. OK. The previous owner's very existence can be expunged via the washing machine or dry cleaner. But an old handbag indelibly bears the marks of Owner Number One's careless biro pen spillage, or the scuff from that day on the tube when they didn't "stand clear of the closing doors," or the stain left on the lining when they hurriedly thrust a half-eaten peach into it as they realised they were about to come face to face with someone they wanted to impress. Clearly the very opposite is true of our Thatcher handbag purchaser. He will eagerly hope for little signs of prime ministerial contact: a spot of stray nail polish, a fingerprint, a hair, some sentimental evidence of Margaret's presence, her firm grip, the aroma of Number 10, or possibly only Number 7.

Of course, it's just as well that we all want to spend our money in different ways. I was in Cheapside last week and popped in to Whittard's Sale. There's generally a nice smell of coffee in Whittards and they sell comfortable, reassuring teapots and dishes, solid-looking and brightly coloured. I noticed that they had bags of pebbles on special offer. Sort of strong mesh bags like they use for onions in bulk. Only smaller. Pebbles of various sizes and shapes and shades. Someone had polished them up a bit. I've never been any good at all at estimating the weight of a fruit cake at village fetes so I may be well adrift, but I guessed there might be three or four kilos of pebbles in each bag. They were priced at £5 the bag. £8 for two, in what seemed to me the unlikely circumstance that anyone could carry more than one. I pictured such a customer staggering back into the office and stowing them under the desk till going-home time. Then gathering them up and perhaps nursing them on the Piccadilly Line in the rush hour. It occurred to me also to wonder what might be the total commercial worth of the beach at, say, Deal, or Lyme Regis, should some enterprising townsperson wish to capitalise on it. I was also reminded of the hours... and hours and hours... I used to spend a few years ago, (or was it fifty?) collecting unusual pebbles and arranging them in a display on the steps of our beach hut at Clacton, to be inspected and admired by the rest of the family. I didn't buy a teapot. Or even a coffee bean.

I must remember to buy some more sultanas. A blackbird family in the hedge outside the kitchen has almost cleaned us out of sultanas. It got to the point when we only had "mixed fruit" left. The glossy-backed gourmets left all the candied peel but the raisins and currants got the thumbs up (in a manner of speaking.) It's been quite an ornithological month really, in the back garden. There are usually at least eight pairs of bluetits in the apple trees, which would be quite delightful if it didn't signal the fact that the trees are covered in aphids. Sparrows seem to be on the increase while the opposite is true of starlings. Magpies are nesting in the conifer next door, while the pigeons favour TV aerials for practically all their activities, or so it seems to me. It was just as well Ellie was in residence recently on the day one of them died under the hebe. She stepped unflinchingly forth with a Sainsbury's disposable carrier and calmly collected the feathery corpse.

Talking of death, I think I am beginning to understand why Grandad Harold derives so much pleasure from the obituary columns. I used to think it was only one-upmanship: the fact that he was still fighting fit at ninety, while the subjects of the articles evidently weren't. I used to think the obituary page was a touch morbid. Well, *very* morbid really. But in fact it isn't at all. It's often intriguing, uplifting and very funny. After all, they wouldn't be likely to devote many inches to someone who had led a quiet blameless life in the suburbs, contentedly avoiding all that might be risky, unorthodox, astounding or infamous! It's generally the other kind they write about. The tribute to John Aspinall, the Zoo man, is a good example. He is reported to have claimed that of his thirty best friends, more than half were animals. Mr. Aspinall evidently went to live in Eaton Square in 1956, with a Capuchin monkey, a nine week old tigress, and two Himalayan bears. Which illustrates my point that the subjects of obituaries are quite often entertaining to read about but not necessarily desirable as neighbours. Another recent entry recorded the death at 94 of The Begum Aga Khan III. Born the daughter of a tram conductor and a seamstress, she later became Miss France and caught the eye of the Aga Khan while dancing the tango at a party given by an Egyptian princess.

Maureen rang this morning with a request: "Are you qualified to sign the back of my passport photo?" Maureen "does" for us. Except when she doesn't. Which is quite often because the nature of her life precludes reliability as normally understood. But, underlying the intermittency of her appearances is a secure understanding that, bad-penny like, she'll turn up again before long. Which suits me fine. An occasional visit from a real cleaning specialist is far preferable to regular ineffective weekly dabbling by a dilettante. Even now, I'm vaguely uncomfortable having someone else hoovering our carpets and Sanilaving our loos. I wasn't born to be "done for." As Maureen announced to her friend, Liz, who accompanied her on the passport foray, "Diana never wanted help in the house. Wanted to do it all herself! Can't of course! Not now! But she likes things looking nice." That's true. And that's certainly what Maureen achieves. The house looks like an annex of the Savoy when she goes, though thankfully she stops short of making little diagonal folds in the bog roll. I don't know what she does with the pillows. They look twice the size after she's made up the beds. Tiles gleam. Order prevails.

But not, according to Maureen, in her own life. Maureen lurches between courses of Prozac and phases of "detoxification." When she's "in detox" I take extra care making myself a guilty cup of coffee and open the kitchen window to waft away the alluring aroma so as not to sabotage her boiled water regime. She does nothing by halves. She enjoys spectacular constipation and whereas other women have "a spot of PMT" Maureen practically miscarries every month. I think perhaps I'm secretly envious that she's the sort of woman who attracts wolf-whistles from labourers on building sites. I don't. I tend to wear loose-fitting clothes to flatter the fact that I'm not a size 10. Maureen favours figure-hugging tightness to make it abundantly clear that she *is*.

Maureen is 40 but looks 30 and has two daughters in their late teens. One is still at school, well technically anyway. She bunks off most of the time and Maureen periodically attends meetings with truancy officers and/or social workers anxious to coax her back into class. The other, older daughter has aspirations to be a pop star. Maureen is generally not very flush with funds. Under the circumstances I thought it would be wise if she were to attract the attention of a tycoon, and advised her thus. Only last week, when everyone else dismissed him as drunk, she gave the kiss of life to a dying diabetic down at The George. I had high hopes that he might be hugely rich, and that his first thoughts on emerging from Whipps Cross Intensive Care Unit would be of the unsqueamish brunette who had launched herself into the profoundly unpleasant task of hauling him back from the brink of eternity. But he turned out to be unemployed and living on long-term incapacity benefit. Maureen's current partner is a penniless painter. They have appalling rows but he buys her bunches of flowers from Walthamstow market (when they are dismantling the stalls and selling them off cheap.)

There's a cliff-edge quality to Maureen's life. Even her reasons for not turning up are not the usual mundanities of "I had a dental appointment" or "The washing machine engineer turned up." Grander far is her canvas: "I was in court about the eviction order." Or "I was lying in bed all day, crying." What do you say to that? In fact what I did say was, "Well, we could *all* do *that*. What a waste of time, you useless woman!" which seemed to cheer her immensely. She was grateful for my lack of sympathy and promised to be around the next week. Even in this matter of the passport Maureen inevitably had to apply at the last possible minute. There's probably only a 50/50 chance that the Petty France Passport office will deliver in time the one essential document she needs for this, her first holiday in ten years.

Grandma Beryl is mass-producing "teddies for tragedies." Beryl is my mother, of course, but now that she has ten grandchildren and the first brace of great grandchildren, Grandma Beryl is the title that suits best. The teddies must conform to a set knitting pattern. They must have fawn or buff-coloured paws and faces, but should otherwise be brightly coloured. The teddies are sent by the thousand to doctors working in the third world or in war-torn countries where they find "children who have their own teddies to cuddle in their cots get better quicker than those who don't have one." Each child keeps his own teddy and can take it home, so the doctors need a continual supply. At the speed Beryl works I should think most of the Eritrean quota is supplied from her needles alone. I've made one bear so far and Ellie rang today to say she's half way up her first trouser leg. Beryl always was one for helping out, especially after we four left home. She was temporarily thwarted after marrying Harold. He was so jealous of any activity that might tax her strength and shorten their years together that no-one but he got a look-in. I suppose if you fall madly in love and marry at 82 you are likely to have a more than usually well-developed protective attitude. After a bit Beryl got wise to his after-lunch naps and was able to slip round undetected to her sightless next-door neighbour to deliver a slice of leftover lemon meringue pie. And with their 10th anniversary fast approaching Harold may be expected to be a tad less possessive. Though I believe he did phone the police last week when she was ten minutes late back from bridge.

It was wonderful to see our niece Alison last week, back from New Zealand, and to share a meal together. Just as well though that she waited till the coffee stage to tell us about the tragic end of a zoo-keeper of her acquaintance who slipped and fell after administering an enema to an elephant. What a way to go! Down Under in more ways than one.

September
Doris took me to "The King and I."

Doris took me to "The King and I" at the London Palladium. Doris is 90, only I'm not supposed to mention it to anyone. She usually wears a velvet hat. I met her in the butcher's last month. At least, I was in the butcher's and she was heading past the butcher's at a purposeful high speed in the direction of Sainsbury's. Doris uses a stick to good effect. Not so much to lean on or to steady herself. More for brandishing. Other pedestrians tend to clear a path. I called out. She changed course instantly and lurched in amongst the steaks and sausages. Dave had already weighed up my kidneys but he sensed an imminent hiatus and moved on temporarily to the next customer.

"Thanks so much for shouting at me," says Doris, a bit out of breath. "I don't hear too well these days. People have to shout. Do you ever manage to get out to the theatre? I'd like to take you. Not next week. In about three weeks. Give me time to book. I'll write to you. Then you can let me know what you want to see."

Doris shouts too. Her normal voice might strike others as a touch dramatic. A wonderful reader in her day, with carrying power even in the open air. So there we were, the two of us, shouting at each other in the butcher's. And everyone knows we are going to the theatre.

It all came to pass as Doris had ordained. Letters were exchanged. We met on South Woodford station at 6.15 p.m. "If we're too early we can look in Liberty's window." I learnt that Doris had gone up twice in person to the box office to get the tickets. I pictured her negotiating all those steps at Oxford Circus. Her "plastic wouldn't work" on the first visit. We sat in the stalls. "You must have the gangway seat!" she insisted. The lights went down. It was all colour and dance and exotic costumes and gorgeous absurdity and "suspended disbelief." And tunes! For a few hours we escaped on the tunes. I did anyway. Doris admitted afterwards she hadn't been able to pick up much as her hearing aid was playing up. (At one point she dropped a small component out of it and I had to crawl about under the seats groping amongst the feet of predominantly sympathetic strangers to rescue it.) But she had seen that I was enjoying every moment, "and *that* was the whole point of the exercise!"

Back on a crowded Oxford Circus platform there were only two seats left for a very necessary recovery phase before the next Epping train, due in twelve minutes. The middle two seats in a clutch of four.

"Do you mind if we join you?" says Doris, gracious as always. She gave no sign of noticing their green hair and pierced eyebrows.

"Of course not. Take a seat!" (She had.) "So long as you don't mind us smoking and being terribly drunk!" He moved the open wine bottle from its precarious position between Doris's sensible shoes.

"Heading home?" she enquired.

"Heading out!" said one.

"The night is young!" said the other. "Why don't you come clubbing with us? You look like a goer!"

They delighted in Doris. Ten minutes' animated conversation passed between equals. The train came in and they waved us off.

We have two telephone lines now, one upstairs and one

down. Not one line with an extension; two separate lines with their own distinct numbers. The upstairs one differs in one digit from the number of the headquarters of a large insurance concern round in Hillcrest Road. Downstairs we share almost the same number as a busy local medical practice. So we get plenty of "wrong numbers." It has even happened that I was in the middle of trying to explain to an upstairs caller why it would be pointless for her to insist on reading out her policy number when I had to hurry down and advise a fretful mother that she was still another call away from getting help for her feverish infant. I'm never irritated by these "wrong numbers." All "visitors" are welcome to visit our enclosed world, however fleetingly. I had such an interesting conversation last Wednesday with a young candidate awaiting the results of his professional insurance institute exams. He'd rung up to ask when he might expect to receive his "brown envelope," but seemed more than happy to talk through his career plans with the total stranger he'd contacted by accident. The sort of private exchanges you have with a fellow traveller on a train when you are confident you'll never meet again.

Wrong numbers unrelated to either insurance or medicine are probably even more intriguing, though I did worry about the fate of poor Mr. Gunawadina stranded at Stanstead Airport when I came in to find an answerphone message from his chauffeur explaining why he wouldn't make the E.T.A. on time after all. I dialled 1471, but "the caller had withheld their number." Last night I took a call from a softly-spoken lady wondering if I had been "talking with her husband about the blue and yellow pressed flowers" an hour or so before. Faced with so charmingly unlikely a scenario I could scarcely reply "Sorry dear, you've dialled the wrong number." Could I? We were soon ranging through hobbies and pastimes various, quite like old friends. But we were no nearer finding out who had been talking to her husband.

When I open my bedroom curtains in the morning it sounds just like someone sneezing. That is, if you hear it from some other part of the house. We discovered this years ago when Auntie Margery came to stay and borrowed my room. Within a day of her arrival I was feeling quite upset on her behalf. "After all those bracing Norfolk breezes, the milder London air and higher pollen count had set off a nasty bout of hay fever." That's what I thought. Until one morning when my entry with her pre-breakfast cuppa coincided with her pulling the curtains. And the truth dawned. Years before, it had been to Auntie Jerry, as she was known, that my older brother David and I were evacuated in 1943 and I slept in a convertible armchair in her front room. We went to the local primary school and Mrs. Maconachie, further up the terrace, taught me how to thread beads. Jerry was warm and kind and left me her piano.

I think I must have struck rather lucky with aunts. Our friends the Hatches had an aunt who was a fervent apostle of total abstinence and would insist on "bearing her witness" at every possible opportunity. She would even rise to her feet at family weddings and rail against the evils of drink just as the assembled guests were on the point of toasting the bride and groom in champagne. It's rather a shame, or perhaps it isn't, that the most vivid memory I have of my Auntie Trixie concerns another sneeze. Trixie's laughter filled a house. She had a gloriously vulgar streak and a conspiratorial giggle. On one occasion she confided in me, all of nine years old, "I've got the sort of sneeze that rots your knickers!" I was shocked and thrilled at the same time. I had thought grown-ups were grown up. It was a wonderful revelation to find that Trixie at least was just a big kid.

When Alastair sneezes, we're not talking about a droll little "Bless you" tickle in the nostrils. We're talking about a deafening "Gesundheit!" rifle blast, a grand scale thunderclap. If you sense that one is imminent, you do well to block your ears. All his old Glyndebourne resonance, every fortissimo in an entire tenor role bursts out in one split second performance. A Wagnerian sneeze. Alastair had a wonderful tenor voice. He trained at the Guildhall School of Music under Joseph Hislop and at the London Opera Centre and was earning a modest living when we first married, singing on stages and in halls up and down the country, including Covent Garden and the Royal Festival Hall. I recall being quite put out watching him in the final dress rehearsal of "Lucia di Lammermoor" at the Wexford Festival one autumn. The baritone upstaged him, waving his cloak up to obscure him in one of his solos. Alastair just chuckled: "Don't worry. It won't happen tonight. I'll focus my first note into his ear." He did. And it didn't. Are you wondering why he left the theatre? He was offered the role of Floristan in Beethoven's "Fidelio" with the Glyndebourne Touring Company. We had been married five years and were thinking how great it would be to have the company of some Junior Newlands.

"What will you be paying me for the role?" he asked the musical director. Shock waves were registered on the Richter Scale over a wide area of Sussex.

"What are you?" was the reply. "A singer or a bloody businessman?"

Thinking about it for a few days, Alastair came to the conclusion that he was "a bloody businessman." As he very successfully turned out to be. The stroke took his voice away as well. He has never again sung a note in tune.

February
I have enrolled for "Beginners' Yoga"

I have enrolled for "Beginners' Yoga," under the auspices of the Waltham Forest Adult Education Programme. It's on a Monday evening at a school near Blackhorse Road tube station. Prompt at 7 30 p.m. hordes of ethnically-varied adults, bent on self-betterment, stream through the reception area before following their own particular tributary. To "Icelandic Poetry" or "Decorative Pottery," "Rudiments of Archaeology" and so forth. It may be a little too soon to say, definitively, but I am fast coming to the conclusion that I probably haven't got what Yoga takes. It's all very well for our instructor. She only weighs about 7 stone. So is it any wonder that she can adopt the cobra position (bhujangasana) or the downward facing dog (adho mukha svanasana) with sickening ease? I'm quite skilled at the corpse posture, in which you lie prostrate and go into deep relaxation. Some of the students have a proper Yoga Mat. I'm quite glad I didn't splash out on one. I'm using a padded coat lining someone gave me for Oxfam, with the armhole bits trimmed off. It does just as well.

You can buy anything these days, can't you. An optimistic trader along the High Road is offering "Balinese and Javanese furniture," on display in his basement showroom. I sometimes wonder what the take-up rate might be. Our greengrocer is selling cartons of "Summer Custard." In the arcade at Liverpool Street yesterday I passed a boutique devoted almost entirely to "exclusive knickers from Brazil." Unfortunately I was in something of a hurry or I might have investigated further. I was en route to Bloomberg, the international news agency, to interview one of their journalists. This was my first visit there, but I hope not my last. Beverages, hot or cold, are usually on offer at offices in the City. But here I was urged to help myself "from the kitchen." And who was I to refuse a plate of fresh raspberries, grapes, water melon and plums? (*After* completing my MORI interview).

I'm not sure I go along with the fashionable insistence on detailed product ingredient information. Only the other day I was on the point of applying some deep-pore-cleansing anti-stress mud pack to my face, (a Christmas tree present), when I noticed it contained "denatured ethanol, glyceryl stearate, fucus vesiculosus and propylparaben."

I got out of bed and walked downstairs yesterday morning and poured a glass of tonic water over the begonias in the porch. I generally offer the begonias what is left in my overnight water glass. I had forgotten that a bottle of tonic had needed using up the night before. The begonias have suffered no ill effects from their dose of quinine. This was only to be expected, since they seem to be virtually indestructible. I have sometimes wondered if they were a hybrid strain, crossed with triffids. They ought to prick my conscience every day when I pass them: I stole their forebear from a pavement tub outside a bungalow in Dufftown, Scotland, about twenty years ago. A spur had been broken off, by a passing postman, possibly, and was lying, doomed, in my path. Probably there is a law relating to damaged tub plants, like the one about clippings from your neighbour's hedge, which must be thrown back over the fence after removal, since they are rightfully theirs. If so I broke it. I put the spur in a polythene bag with some water and brought it home and, like the feral cats we have been hearing about from the RSPCA this week, it has produced prodigious numbers of offspring and proved impervious to frost, drought, starvation, and even tonic water.

Gordon has just sent me an email about a competition in the Washington Post. Contestants had to supply alternative dictionary definitions for well-known words. Amongst my favourites from the winning entries were :

Flabbergasted (adj.): appalled at how much weight you have gained.

Gargoyle (n.): an olive-flavoured mouthwash.

Balderdash (n.): a rapidly receding hairline.

I have been exhibiting mild symptoms of bereavement over the past week attributable to the collapse of my email facility. This is plainly absurd. A friendly technician named Terry turned up on Monday in a red baseball cap worn back-to-front and replaced the "motherboard." What a mercy Alastair had insisted on a 5 year warranty for our Apricot. I was on tiptoe of expectation when he left, to scan the scores of waiting messages. There was only a flier from Nationwide and some special offers from Freeserve. I dispatched one of my own immediately to my brother Michael. He lives in Barbados. I know he'll reply at once and bring gusts of breezy tropical air into our centrally-heated suburban London home. Email is a beautiful bonus for computer owners. But I hope it won't ever completely kill off letters by post. Which reminds me that I must check something out with you: I hope I am right in assuming that you have all realised there is no necessity, ever, to go into a stationery shop and buy a rubber band. I don't want to offend you by stating the obvious, but a short stroll in the wake of your average postman will ensure a good year's supply. Strong, of superior quality, and cost-free. A tactic of admirable prudence, with worthwhile open-air exercise thrown in as a secondary plus-point. Not only that but you will be helping to keep Britain tidy and playing a modest part in the still very fashionable trend towards recycling. I'm not altogether certain why Royal Mail has not been brought to court by the Department of the Environment for this widespread flouting of the litter laws. But till that happens there's no reason why the rest of us shouldn't clean up, in more ways than one, is there?

June

The municipal dump was more than usually crowded today

The municipal dump was more than usually crowded today. It was a fine day and people had been able at last to get at their gardens with spades and secateurs; throw open their windows and look through more minimalist eyes at the accumulated clutter of winter in their homes. I'm not familiar with any nudist beaches but I picture them as places of cheerful camaraderie. Self-consciousness abandoned along with the clothes. No-one caring what anyone else thinks. The freedom to look pretty damn funny along with everyone else. It was a bit like that at the dump this morning. Not that anyone was padding back and forth to the bins in the buff. But the sheer volume of redundant possessions being hurled away seemed to produce an almost carnival atmosphere of neighbourly merriment. No-one minded being seen carting rusty fireguards, broken chairs, tatty old carpets, cracked lavatory seats, to offer up on the community heap. Elderly ladies with neat grey buns in their hair carrying complete bushes over their heads to toss into the garden refuse corner. (A long-overdue addition to our "civic amenity site.") Mattresses, sinks, pictures. The dump "operatives" egging everyone on: "Let's be having you, mate. Give us it here, ducks." A shared celebration of the whole jettisoning process, joy unbounded. Even, increasingly now, a multi-ethnic flavour with citizens of all colours and creeds uniting in the festive ambiance of disposal on a grand scale and the sheer physical satisfaction of chucking stuff away.

I believe the borough department responsible for refuse collection, recycling and rubbish dumping is known as "Cleansing Services." They look after borough conveniences as well. Really rather a fun department altogether. I don't think I have updated you regarding Alastair's longstanding relationship with the "Trees on Highways" department. This finally bore fruit a month or so ago. In fact it ended up with Alastair having a direct line through to Mr Leeming at the Town Hall "Trees on Highways" department because he was so often being put through by mistake to "Trees in Parks" or sometimes "Trees on Private Land Encroaching on the Highway" which led to some quite unnecessarily long-winded and uncongenial exchanges. On one occasion he even spent some time explaining his arboreal business to "Trespassing Bye-laws," (next on the switchboard's alphabetical list, presumably,) before the mistake was rectified and the pathway cleared. The friendly telephonist in some desperation decided to grant him a short cut. Mr Leeming and his colleague, Mr Marshall, are by now very familiar with Alastair's Scottish accent and with his championship of the environment. They have been on the receiving end of pleasantly periodic calls from him since the day a parcel delivery van reversed into the ornamental malus on the pavement outside number 31. It was a hit and run incident. The van driver quit the scene leaving the infant tree mortally wounded. Within minutes it had become, I suppose, the responsibility of the "Unimpeded Access to Public Paths" department, and later it was tossed up into a borough truck, without ceremony. But at least one citizen mourned its fate. Alastair insisted on ringing Redbridge daily. The "new," paralysed Alastair is given to obsessions. One early one was the desire for a chaise longue on which he might recline. We drove all the way to Luton one weekend, to the High Seat Company and chose a suitable sofa. But he never sits in it. He feels uneasy and insecure out of his wheelchair. The provision of a fresh "municipal" tree was a more recent obsession. And that's why at 9 38. one morning in March - I recall we had just remarked that at least half the pedestrians passing the window were either on the phone or eating their breakfast, or both - Lewis from Ilford, and Jan (pronounced Yan), from Poland, drew up in a sort of huge cage on wheels and lifted down the long-promised replacement. First there was some preliminary turning of the soil, then the lowering of the prunus pandora into its prepared niche. By this time we were out on the pavement offering grateful encouragement, cups of tea, advice regarding vertical alignment, and so forth. And Alastair was presented with the identity tag and details of a recommended programme of watering and feeding for the tree in its formative years. "It's your tree now, mate."

None of you will be surprised to hear that I have ducked out of the yoga classes while I still have any trouble-free joints. This must be chalked up as a failure, I know. But right back in my school history classes when we learnt about the Inquisition and such like, I feared that I would never be able to stand torture, certainly not for two hours on end. This leaves me with the task of finding an alternative course for Monday evenings. And therein lies the rub: whereas most people look for their chosen subject and arrange to attend the classes at the published times, I have to start from the fact that it must be on a Monday evening, when I have agency "care" scheduled. I have scoured the Evening Institutes for miles around, the libraries, colleges, Community Associations, the lot. Monday isn't a favourite slot for evening class teachers. As far as I can see, Criminology, Beginners' Spanish, Forestry Techniques and Rock Climbing are my only choices, unless I fancy a degree in Electrical Engineering or Hotel Management. I'd like to try my hand at Drawing for Beginners, and I gave serious thought to a "life class" somewhere in Barking. But without the skill to draw so much as a chimney or a toadstool, the thought of attempting to do justice to the tones and lines and lumps and bumps and beauty of the human form was too terrifying to take further. As the evenings are long and light I could possibly take a notebook out and construct a series of "Woodford Walks" with notes on landmarks, and anecdotes about local worthies and supermarkets. Or I could get on my bike, and check out the user-friendliness of the latest crop of cycle lanes hereabouts, with thoughtful suggestions on how to proceed when, all of a sudden, they disappear.

August
I had to get out of bed at three o'clock this morning to kill a mosquito.

I had to get out of bed at three o'clock this morning to kill a mosquito. Presumably mosquitoes would have an improved life expectancy if they kept quiet. It's surprising that they haven't evolved into silence. Currently they are still saddled with the audible-warning handicap, tilting the odds slightly in favour of their intended victim. Having said that, my 3 a.m. adversary had probably got to me before I got to him because he made a bit of a red stain on my new cream carpet which I had to wash off first thing today. Cold water did the job. I read somewhere that Dr. Albert Schweitzer's central philosophy, his "reverence for life," absolutely precluded the destruction of any other living thing, however unattractive, however potentially harmful. Apparently he forbade the killing of mosquitoes even in the operating theatre, which must have been a considerable inconvenience to his surgical team. (Presumably he didn't use disinfectant either, which would have disposed of unseen bugs by the billion.) Anyway, I killed my mosquito with a clear conscience, irreverent or not, slept well and felt maximum relief and minimum remorse.

I've got "bilberry" walls in my bedroom now. From the

139

Crown Covermatt Eggshell range, ("low odour, low taint"). Mike next door says all the colours are exactly the same as they ever were but the manufacturers change their names every so often to make you think you're bang up to date. Of course, being a police officer in constant close communication with the criminal fraternity, he does seem to have a more than usually glum view of human nature. I've admitted to him on several occasions that I have to be feeling strong to engage in any long conversations with him as he always leaves me with the feeling that virtually nothing is as it seems. But there's no doubting the fact that he is kindness itself and regularly mows our front lawn, even strimming the edges with his new petrol-driven strimmer. I can assure you: "that's when neighbours become good friends."

My friendly blackbird is now known as Billy, for obvious alliterative reasons. I call his wife Mrs. Billy, which is completely crass and unimaginative and anti-feminist too, I suppose. I'm inclined to be slightly displeased with Billy. He has been eating me out of sultanas for several years now and I was grateful to find some remarkably cheap Californian raisins at the greengrocer's a few weeks ago. A kilo pack for only £1.25. (Our greengrocer is the sort of greengrocer who sells multi-packs of toilet rolls, Imperial Leather soaps, Robertson's strawberry jam, Colgate toothpaste etc. And raisins. Anything he can get hold of at a bargain price, basically, to supplement his profits on bananas and cabbages.) There can be no acceptable reason why Billy should turn his beak up at these raisins. They are full of rich flavour, sticky and swollen. But whereas he flaps about at the kitchen window till I decant a few sultanas on to the garden table, and scoffs them four at a time within ten minutes, he is demonstrating regrettable finickiness over the raisins. He eventually forces them down just before dusk, when it's clear I'm not going to indulge his presumptuous whims. By the way, did you read that, in the first frenzy of announcements for the candidature in the Tory Party Leadership race, Ken

Clarke was said to be "bird-watching in Vietnam"? Lord Archer must have been green with envy: so improbable a story, but universally believed and probably true!

The story I get on the majority of occasions when I ring Gordon or Ellie is that they have "just finished a long run." Or a middle or short distance run. "Personal bests" have been shattered. The combined aura of fitness and sweat filters down the phone line. Another race entered and run, sometimes even won. Alastair was the South of Scotland 800 metre champion in an earlier lifetime. He didn't have much luck on the horses yesterday. The one advantage of this is that I only had to go down to William Hills once. The district nurse who called in this afternoon to measure Alastair's inside leg, for reasons I needn't bore you with, confessed to something of an addiction to a flutter, dating from a period of in-hospital service on a "Men's Surgical Ward."

"All activity stopped when the race was on," she told us, "with everyone glued to the nearest telly and shouting and cheering."

Inevitably, I found myself picturing a long double row of beds on either side of your typical NHS ward, with bandaged fists punching the air, and howls of disappointment or triumph mixed up with post-operative groans. And from a far corner a plaintive cry, unheard, as High and Mighty romped home, "Can somebody *please* bring me a bed pan!"

Alastair's most loyal, long-term carer recently expressed to me the view that time doesn't always move at the same pace. And he wasn't talking about the well-known fact that our forefathers, centuries ago, counted dawn to dusk as twelve hours and dusk to dawn as another twelve hours, so that, obviously, the daytime hours of summer were longer than the night-time hours. And the reverse in winter. No, Geoffrey feels that the sense that Life is passing more quickly as you get older is not altogether an illusion. I'm not sure what happens when an octogenarian spends a day with a two year old. But, be that as it may, I do subscribe to the view

141

that the journey to somewhere you haven't been to before always takes longer than the journey back home again. The route can be exactly the same, even the journey "time" identical. But it's "quicker."

I had the simplest of opportunities to test this theory on my First Great Western train to Padstow recently, when it occurred to me in the vicinity of Taunton that a fresh cup of coffee was essential to my survival. I set off in search of the buffet car. Was there a buffet car? Would they have any hot water? (Last time I travelled to Scotland it was "Cold drinks only, dear.") I left Coach B, passed through C, D, E and F, lurching between munching, snoozing, chatting, crosswording passengers, some with protruding limbs requiring to be stepped over, others with carelessly stowed luggage cluttering up the aisle. The buffet car eventually materialised. The buffet car attendant lacked humour but the coffee was good. The return route to Coach B: well, I scarcely noticed it. Coming from the unknown back to the known. There in rapid view was my, by now, familiar fellow traveller, the contract sheep-shearer from New Zealand, scribbling long overdue letters to friends in the Antipodes. (I heard all about her when she asked to borrow a biro. Hers had run out.) There too was the irrepressible 18 month old Ellis with his mother in the other four-seater opposite, chatting to his reflection every time we passed through a tunnel or shadowy cutting, then hunting for it when all he could see was the sun and the sea or a field of contented cows. All around the carriage, eyes were trained on Ellis, mesmerised by his contentment. Hoping it was contagious perhaps. Or wishing they were back in the days when life went by at his more andante tempo.

It's probably my fault: I should have separate fridges for the black olives and the canned prunes. It's the second time it's happened. I was just too late this morning to stop the overnight carer from handing Alastair his Shreddies topped with olives. "I did think they were rather small prunes," she said. "Yes, and smooth and circular and definitely savoury," I might have said, but I didn't. I generally prefer to avoid confrontation. It isn't as if Alastair enjoys olives, even with his sun-dried tomatoes, spinach leaves and mozzarella.

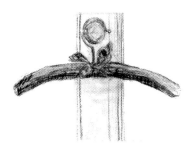

January

This has been a prodigiously good winter for spiders' webs.

This has been a prodigiously good winter for spiders' webs. Best viewed at first light, heavy with dew, on one of those low, streaky sun mornings, and (if you'll pardon the Bellamy-esque exuberance,) looking for all the world as if Titania had dropped her entire collection of necklaces in haste to fly home for breakfast before Oberon had polished off all the sausages. One of Alastair's nightshirts got left outside on the rotary clothes line right round the clock last Wednesday. Don't go imagining a common or garden pale blue striped winceyette affair, ordered from an undies catalogue and slightly faded from frequent washing. No, this was one of Alastair's luxury viyella nightshirts, made to measure for him in India and brought back by our generous neighbour opposite. By Thursday morning it had become the lynchpin, or cornerstone of approximately sixteen fresh webs. The right-angled spaces between the arms and the main body had proved to be the most popular locations, the Mayfair or Park Lane of the arachnid property world, with Bond Street and Piccadilly round the head hole, slightly vulnerable to perching pigeons, while the Old Kent Road and Whitechapel were down at the hemline, where a casual flick of Phoebe's tail could demolish whole webby homesteads in a few indifferent seconds.

Regrettably - tragically you might say - the shirt had to be unpegged and brought in to defrost. The washing cycle cannot even under such poignant circumstances, be allowed to grind to a halt. Especially this week, when one of Alastair's only three winter-weight nightshirts has vanished. And it is his dearly-loved deep-crimson tartan number. If, as seems most likely, it has been swallowed up in the Whipps Cross Hospital laundry system, the entire supply of in-patient sheets will probably be stained pink by the end of the week. The safe return of the tartan to Room 2 on Sycamore Ward will be my urgent challenge, but I suspect it will be a challenge of Anneka Rice proportions. Success is by no means guaranteed. Whipps Cross Hospital is huge. There are just over 800 beds. So it is something of an enigma as to why the daily tally of 1,600 sheets, pillow slips, towels, blankets and nightwear should have to trundle down the A12 to be processed at humble Goodmayes Hospital. Presumably Alastair's nightshirt, instead of coming home with me, has by this time made the return trip to Goodmayes three times, hung around in traffic jams, and been offered each day to startled sufferers in Patience Ward or perhaps Hope, in spite of Alastair's bold woven name tag on the breast pocket.

You will have gathered that Alastair has been "hospitalised." He fell down in the bathroom on my weekly evening out and fractured his femur. I am spending four to six hours daily at the hospital and we are now in the twenty-second week. The orthopaedic surgeon says it is too dangerous to operate so Alastair is in traction. And in frequent pain. The leg is not healing. It's a nightmare.

My reflexologist is moving to the Isle of Wight, to a fisherman's cottage near Bembridge Harbour. I include this piece of information, which can be of no possible interest to any of you, because it has a nice airy out and about feel to it. More bracing than the details of intravenous fluids, blocked catheters, traction pins, pressure sores, nebulizers, enemas and indeterminate soups that make up an average day's programme on Sycamore Ward.

Queues can be good places to chat. Yesterday was Tuesday, so my brother David had called in to the ward for his weekly visit with Alastair, leaving me free to nip down to the shops. I was soon swapping experiences over the cabbages at Harvey's with a woman whose mother has also been "hospitalised."

"I hate that word!"she erupted, "Hospitalised!"

I was quite concerned about the "spit" element as we were by then passing the display of lettuces. But what a treat to bump into another silly old-fashioned purist like me. Passing the potatoes and parsnips we dissected BT's nasty automated 1471 message "You were called today at 11 55 a.m. The caller (singular) withheld *their* (plural) number." I checked out that she had spotted the split infinitive on the Boots Vitamin Pills canister: "It can be difficult with today's hurried lifestyle *to always eat* a balanced diet." And of course, by the time it was our turn for Peter, the greengrocer's customary greeting, "Hello gorgeous," we were chewing over that choicest of London Underground curiosities, "All trains are not stopping at Bank Station."

Incidentally, before we leave the greengrocer's, his eggs are enormous. Did you read those reports of recent research into the dimensions of eggs? Apparently, chickens "lay bigger eggs when they smell a foul odour." I recall absorbing this fact on the Circle Line en route to Farringdon. I'd picked up a copy of the "Metro" and spent the remainder of my journey trying to visualise what kind of controlled experimentation and assessment techniques could possibly have yielded this conclusion. How many chickens took part? Was it a random sample? How were other potentially biasing factors eliminated? Was there a clutch of cloned cockerels available to rule out genetic variations? Were some hens subjected to periodic wafts of Chanel Number 5 and others exposed to relentless stench? The greengrocer's supplier must house his hens next to a sewage works.

It was good to read that the Queen and her Mama regularly attend meetings of the Sandringham Women's Institute. The Queen Mother had to give it a miss last week as she had a cold. But the Queen was able to admire "members' home-baked shortbread and decorated padded coathangers." So reassuringly the sort of thing one expects of the W.I. Not like that other lot who took off all their clothes and posed in the nude for a calendar. Tastefully though, while arranging flowers or whipping up a Victoria sponge. And they did raise hundreds of thousands of pounds, I believe. And started quite a trend.

You can either make a Victoria sponge or you can't. Mine turn out like crisp pancakes, scarcely half an inch thick even when the two halves are sandwiched together with dollops of butter cream. It's probably quite important to get used to what it feels like to fail. As early in life as possible. School Sports Days afforded me many opportunities over the years. I was in the ball-throwing competition once. I was six. The others had mastered the over-arm method but I was still stuck with under-arm. A mixture of enthusiasm and dread caused me to swing the throwing arm too far before releasing the ball with the result that it disappeared into a garden adjoining the playground, some long distance behind me. In my running heat, (we went off in fours,) I can still hear the teacher stationed at the tape proudly calling out, "First…Second…Third!" I came next. "Was I fourth?" I asked. Now, here was her opportunity. She shouldn't have smiled. She should have said, "No dear, you were last! The others were all better than you. You may be good at joined-up writing and walking round with a bean bag on your head, but when it comes to running, you are a failure, useless, bottom of the heap."

Remembering numbers is another area of weakness. Many's the time I have stood on one of those specially chosen draughty pavement sites with my plastic card in my hand and a cash point beaming a message of welcome, but with no hope of recollecting my P.I.N code. Car numbers are worse, with their mix of letters and numerals. Alastair used to have a car called MUD. I saw quite an impressive one at the Green Man roundabout yesterday: PLC. But I preferred the one parked, as it happened, outside the hospital renal unit: UPU. I've got seven friends for supper this evening. One of them has just rung to say that mushrooms give her food poisoning, It's OK. I'm doing shepherd's pie. I haven't started to peel the potatoes yet. Must go. Much love.

PS. Did you know that when you look up "Searching" in the Microsoft Word Guide, it says "See Finding"? Optimistic, aren't they!

Eight weeks after this letter was written, Alastair was finally offered an operation to pin his broken leg. It would provide his only hope of ever coming home again. Accepting the risk, he underwent surgery. He died five days later.

Extract from just one of all the letters sent to me:

"For me, Alastair slipped his moorings suddenly in May seven years ago and had been adrift in a fog with …one very large tug boat trying to stop him slipping further away… I must try to remember Alastair only prior to this event… He was so calm externally at our last meeting prior to the operation next day, that I could say, 'See you next Wednesday.' And perhaps for me it was the best visit to remember him in his hospital cell.

Diana, you have now to fill the empty space in your life and fill it you must, because you have lost what has been your all-consuming activity of the post-stroke years. I hope you will be able to look to those who have helped and sustained you through this period. You are in my prayers…and I do not see a blank wall but an open space."

Keith

January
A year has passed. Forgive the long silence

A year has passed. Forgive the long silence. Nothing could have prepared us for the pain and nothing can be said.

With no sign of my elusive "comic muse" (as one of your Christmas letters put it) reappearing voluntarily, I made a resolution at New Year to go in serious and earnest search of her. I have spent most of today with my MORI hat on, talking to people in Wales. With addresses like 43 Cwrt Ty Fferm, Llanbradach. Oddly enough the lady who lived there was called Jennifer. She'd lived there for a year and still wasn't quite sure how to pronounce it. Before that, she told me, they'd lived in Germany at 12 Achtungweidenstrasse, Schwabmunchen. She couldn't pronounce that either, even after three years. The sooner she moves to Park Lane the better, I thought. Or, failing that, the Old Kent Road.

We didn't get out the Monopoly Board this Christmas, so we avoided the seething tensions and prolonged, grim confrontations that constitute its main attraction. It was good to be reassured during our afternoon walk that silly party games are alive and well in South Woodford. From time to time a glimpse was caught of families in mid charade, or cavorting noisily about in unusual clothing or deep in thought, in a circle, paper and pencil in hand, no doubt trying to think of a river beginning with V or a fruit beginning with F. Back at number 31, the twenty-objects-on-a-tray game proved unexpectedly popular, and obsessed more than half the party for at least an hour or so, while the roast potatoes were reaching perfection. This memory exercise had to be repeated so many times, by unanimous request, that small portable items were being plundered from drawers and cupboards all over the house to cope with demand. Later on, six solemn faces wearing paper hats could be seen squashed round a card table trying to catalogue the contents of a pillow case containing some cunningly similar objects, a candle, an empty tube of Smarties etc. At least, I had hoped they were cunningly similar. But everyone got full marks. At 1.45 in the morning, any passers-by might have stopped to stare at the stalwart residue of the party addressing one another as vegetables while keeping their teeth strictly out of sight. A challenging occupation. And at 1.45 in the morning, surprisingly hilarious.

I should probably update you about some significant developments of the past year. The paperboy has grown another foot. A local property consortium is trying to persuade us that a huge complex of apartments and public restaurants and a swimming pool at Gates Corner are what we have all been waiting for. For years. "George Gate: a gateway to a better South Woodford". It seems they want to "revitalise us" and give us "a positive economic boost." Meanwhile, at least two small fashion boutiques are at the everything-must-go stage, one having only recently come, whereas the fingernail painting business down by the station is constantly crammed with customers while hopefuls who forgot to book an appointment are queuing outside and getting mixed up with the clientele at Andy's fruit stall.

A boy at our church has just won his height in pizzas. What a coup! All he did was buy a pizza and the shop gave him a raffle ticket and his number came up. There is a picture of him in the local Guardian with a tower of boxes. Pepperoni and pineapple, gruyere and wild mushroom, bacon, tomato and red onion. You name it. I'm glad they don't mention his brother's comment, "Pity it wasn't me!" His brother is at least twelve pizzas taller. They don't mention either whether the pizzas must be claimed immediately or can be collected from the shop on a gradual basis, as required. "Pop down and get a pizza, dear. Don't feel like cooking tonight. Hands up for savoury tuna and broccoli. Anyone for pork sausage and leek?" If the prize lapses after a period, like a lottery win, and he must take immediate delivery of the final foot or two of pizzas or forfeit the lot, what is going to happen to all the frozen peas and chicken breasts and pick-your-own raspberries and Iceland 20 for the price of 16 profiteroles in the family freezer?

The number of sharks in the North Atlantic has more than halved in the past year. I read that in the Telegraph. I've only once flown over the North Atlantic, on a brief but gloriously memorable trip with Alastair to Seattle. The North Atlantic is very large. And it's difficult to picture sharks lining up for an orderly census, like when Quirinius was Governor of Syria. Of course I believed it about the sharks, because that's what it said in the Telegraph. But how did they count them? Who went down and totted them up? Reminds me of a hysterical day in the school holidays once when Gordon, Ellie and I took ourselves over to Enfield High Street with click-counters to record the number of cars per hour passing through. I can't remember now who was employing us. The Council, I suppose. Wondering whether to "pedestrianise" the shopping centre. But to return to the sharks. The researchers must have developed sonar mathematics or something. It used to be just Pure or Applied when I was at Woodford High. Not that I ever found it pure unless you mean pure purgatory. And certainly I couldn't see that it applied to anything. Although it is surprising these days to find check-out ladies reeling from shock when you hand them the right money, all totted up, for the eight items in your basket. In my schooldays you were "Arts" or

"Sciences," Wordsworth or Bunsen burners, and never the twain shall meet. Give me a nice iambic pentameter and I'm on firm ground. But scientific data on shark populations, that's where I confess I'm all quicksand and mire.

March
A rat has been squatting in next door's Wendy House

A rat has been squatting in next door's Wendy House. His presence was not welcome and indeed I can report that after months of playing cat and mouse with Melanie, my intrepid neighbour, the rat is no longer squatting but resting in peace in a shallow grave under the left-hand plum tree. Unless of course one of the many visiting foxes has dug him up and reintroduced him to the food chain. The rat often used to pop into the compost bin for a bit of extra warmth. On several occasions when Melanie lifted the lid to chuck in a load of carrot peelings, she found herself eyeballing the cosy rodent. Not that she lingered long before slamming the lid back on and retreating to the kitchen to consult yet again her leaflet on rat elimination techniques. Whatever technique she stuck with finally paid off. On the subject of rats I'm confident you all heard about someone's assessment (The Ministry of Health? David Bellamy?) that we are all, always, within ten feet of a rat. Or is it ten yards? I read an extraordinary article last week about John Tull and his wife, Lucinda, well-to-do Americans in mid life enjoying a hiking holiday, who contracted bubonic plague in New Mexico. Apparently the rats in those parts carry the disease and then it is transmitted via fleas to humans. As it was post September 11th, they were immediately mistaken for bio-terrorists. But not for long. Fortunately for them a New York doctor specialising in "travel medicine" recognised their terrible sores as "buboes" and managed to save their lives, just about, though not John's feet. You've got to admire this Mr. Tull. He may have lost his feet, but certainly not his sense of humour and zest for life. After 60 days in a coma his philosophy is splendidly up-beat. He is looking forward to being out and about on his new legs, and dismisses the episode as "a million to one happenstance."

Happenstance! What can you say to that? It reminds me of a quotation Alastair was very fond of about England and America being "two countries divided by a common language." I looked up the quotation in the Oxford Dictionary of Quotations and found it was evidently a "misquotation," attributed to George Bernard Shaw but "not found anywhere in his published writings." Surely he might have just spoken it. At a party, perhaps. He lived long enough to have said an awful lot of things, and if he repeated them often enough which he well could have done (he was 94 when he died) plenty of his pals could have remembered it. Still, I followed the instruction in the ODQ which said "See under Wilde." Oscar, I found, went into print with: "We have really everything in common with America nowadays, except, of course, language." The trouble is Wilde went into print with so much wonderful stuff there are four whole columns of it in the ODQ that you can't help glancing at: "I never travel without my diary. One should always have something sensational to read on the train."

"I can resist everything, except temptation."

"A man cannot be too careful in the choice of his enemies." Don't pick up the ODQ if you're behind schedule! I knew Bob Hope was famous for his remark, "Well, I'm still here!" after his death had been erroneously reported and tributes paid to him in Congress. But I didn't know he said,

"A bank is a place that will lend you money if you can prove that you don't need it." (Incidentally, I still vividly recall a meeting I attended at university, with a guest speaker from the National Spiritualists League. And he called up George Bernard Shaw from the next world, where he was still rabbiting away. So, possibly, the Anglo-American observation *was* his, perhaps even a little gobbet of his *posthumous* wit.)

Another impossibly time-consuming activity is "sorting out the videos." I made a long-planned start yesterday evening. Intentions good: Check out which videos actually contain what is written on the label. Put in re-use pile those with no further interest. Reject the ones that cut off ten minutes before the end (thanks to helpful modern video-technology). The ones where we never know who dunnit or who will live happily ever after with whom. These are merely a source of anguish. No-one wants to hear *your* version of Alec Guinness blowing up the Kwai Bridge, or Braveheart being hung, drawn and quartered. And definitely not a verbal account of how Darcy finally (once they were safely wed,) kissed his Elizabeth. After an hour or so, when I was about a quarter the way through a lovely old version of The Go-between, I remembered that that wasn't what I set out to do, and switched it resolutely off. But it was time for bed anyway. I'd only "sorted out" four videos. About 150 to go.

In the same room as the videos there is an extra large hat box. Octagonal and striped in black and white. I don't have any extra large hats. This box is big enough to accommodate one of those My Fair Lady creations. But it had such a sophisticatedly silly, Noel Coward nonsense look about it that I rescued it from the top shelf above the ladies' coats rack in the Cancer charity shop next to the butcher's. It looked out of place amongst the slightly frayed lamp-shades, the old-style luggage (without wheels), the once-loved but now discarded bathroom cabinets and so forth. Like a lobster thermidor lurking amongst the bacon butties at one of those

24 hour "caffs" in motorway lay-bys. At the time I had no idea what to do with the hat box. No long-term plans beyond affording it the respect so obviously due. But now I am filling it full of rubbish. Not rubbish as in damp tea bags, kipper bones or the drippy seeds from the centres of melons. But rubbish as in junk. The initiated amongst you will immediately recognise the term "junk" as a technical term for some of the most vital ingredients in modern primary education. The Cinderellas of ordinary domestic life with the potential to become the princesses of the classroom. Take the tube at the centre of your average toilet roll. Crying out to be carefully bisected, painted red, and inserted as the funnels in a model of, say, the Waverley paddle steamer. The centre of a kitchen paper roll might readily convert to a factory chimney, and plant the first seeds of ambition to rid the world of pollution in the dribbly-nosed mind of a four-year old at his playstation. The ring that is left when you finish the sellotape. The reels with no cotton. The pleasingly dome-shaped caps from used up roll-on deodorants. All undeniably the raw materials of creativity in the gluey fingers of the latest intake of recruits in the "reception" class. Stretching their intellects, developing their dexterity and manual skills, firing their imaginations etc. (Or even just keeping them contentedly occupied, and not "Please Miss-ing" for a briefly blissful five minutes).

I'd love to be more web-literate. (Well, if "happenstance" is a word....!) I feel I'm probably missing out on all that searching around amongst the dot coms. I nearly always get lost, and feel all inadequate and frustrated and overwhelmed by a bombardment of information about everything in the world except the thing I wanted to find out about. I usually trot off down to the companionable local library instead. Much better exercise and there's something about having a book in your hands. If you've read any good ones lately please do send me titles and authors. By email if you like. Though I still prefer envelopes that drop on the doormat.

I received one today. It was a customer satisfaction questionnaire from the crematorium as a follow-up to Uncle Bert's funeral. A modestly elegant "best value" response form to be completed and then folded, three ways, in accordance with the diagrammatic instructions, then moistened round the edge-flaps, pressed to seal, and dispatched. No stamp required. Printed in black and white with pale lilac sub headings. Quite tall. Will-shaped, really. Not your average sort of mailing: like the Plumbs loose-cover sale catalogue, or the Readers' Digest sweepstake or the phone bill. No, this was truly something on which to exercise the mind.

"How do you normally travel to the crematorium?" Normally! As if one were commuting on a regular basis.

"Did any of those attending the service have any difficulty in finding their way to the correct chapel?" On balance, there seemed little point in outlining the problems of one posse of relations who did have difficulty, not in finding the right chapel but in finding the right crematorium. Regrettably, they appeared just a few minutes late. But those few minutes were crucial. Their arrival immediately followed the coffin's departure. The curtains had already inched their respectful way round Bert's brass-handled box. Non-arrival at funerals is probably endemic hereabouts: The City of London crematorium, Manor Park, is not far, as the crow flies, from the Manor Park crematorium. But by road it's another matter entirely. It's all too easy to get confused. And you can't very well request an encore for latecomers. The curtains re-opening and the coffin trundling back in. Sort of instant reincarnation.

"Have you any views on the toilet facilities at the chapels?" I left this one blank.

"Was the role of the chapel attendant helpful to the proceedings?" In a word, no. But I elaborated: In bitterly cold conditions, the attendant had refused to allow our waiting crowd of mostly elderly mourners to enter the warm, deserted chapel, just four minutes before our designated time-slot, on the grounds that we'd all have to be turned out again if the undertaker failed to show up with the body. I asked if our particular undertaker, who came strongly recommended, had ever been known to miss the deadline, so to speak. But by then, the attendant had hurried inside to keep warm.

"There is current technology available that will allow heat recovered from the cremation process to provide heating for the chapels. Would you find this proposal objectionable?" Something to ponder over indeed! Not over the principle of the thing of course. We children of the recycling age could scarcely take exception to such an intelligently eco-friendly stratagem. But rather over the nature of the available "current technology." Current, hinting at something new. Technology suggestive of micro chips and computer wizardry. But I would have thought pipes had been pretty standard equipment for centuries.

The finale: "Would you like to be involved in our Cemetery Feedback Group?" A winsome plea: "Do let's keep in touch. We know cemeteries aren't bread and butter to you but they are to us so please come back and tell us how you think we are doing." Who knows? Perhaps it was at just such a feedback group that successful policy changes were hatched. Policies that led to the much coveted accolade, "Cemetery of the Year 2001." I noticed this printed boldly on the receipt when I paid for the urn. How had this honour been achieved? On what criteria? Presumably there are only so many prettiest villages in Essex to inspect in an average year. Do the same panels of judges fill up their fallow periods strolling round graveyards with their clipboards, awarding points for an extra-clean catacomb and a well-swept vault, high quality plastic grass matting and tenderly pruned memorial roses?

June
Letters need to brew, like tea.

Letters need to brew, like tea. You can't just pour them out, without first drawing the maximum flavour from whatever assorted tea bags are to hand. And you can't always expect Fortnum's Earl Grey to be available. As likely as not it'll be Tesco Brown Label quality. (But every little helps!) My first 'tea bag' this month is tomato ketchup. I strolled into the quadrangle at Bancroft's School this morning en route to the chapel for the 11 a.m. service, when a piece of cardboard came blowing round the corner and into my face. Litter is so rare in this particular location that I naturally inspected the piece of cardboard and read the following message: "We are sorry there is no tomato ketchup today." In capitals actually, and in red. Clearly a matter of considerable importance and regret. Last time I looked there were at least 8 to 10 different brands of tomato ketchup on the shelves of Sainsbury's so it's not easy to see how one could run out of the stuff. I pictured the groans and gnashing of teeth on the part of ketchup-deprived Bancroft's pupils, if, as I supposed, the notice had been pinned to the dining hall doors on Friday. Anyway, as it was Christian Aid Week and thoughts were rightly turning to the plight of those with no clean water let alone tomato ketchup, the degree of sympathy evoked was minimal.

My second equally unlikely tea bag this month was a mobile phone on the pavement outside the local undertaker's. People were stepping over it or looking away or "passing by on the other side." I did too. Then I went back. The phone was bright pink. Given its location I inevitably pondered over the fact that "we brought nothing into this world and it is certain we can carry nothing out." But as the proportion of the undertaker's customers with bright pink phones must be relatively small I veered towards two alternative explanations: either that it had been thrown away, disposed of, in the manner of those little pyramids of cigarette stubs some drivers, idling at traffic lights, have decided to "tidy out" from their ash tray, or that it had been carelessly dropped. I had by this time picked up the phone and noted that there was some faint text visible on the screen. I couldn't read it because I hadn't got my glasses on. But the second explanation now seemed more likely. I pictured a teenager, female, not yet aware of the panic about to engulf her. I pocketed the phone and took it home. It was rather low on charge so I plugged it in and awaited the call from the frenzied fifth former. Sure enough, she rang. And rang off again almost at once. Thought she'd dialled the wrong number. But she rang again. All was soon made plain. It was "her boyfriend's phone." How wonderful. That which they did not know he had lost had already been found. I left the phone, recharged, in the porch, and went out to choir practice. On my return it had metamorphosed into a box of Cadbury's Milk Tray with a scribbled note: "Thank you for finding my phone. I'd be lost without it! Mark." And that's the truth. I only say that because several of you seemed to think I had invented the cemetery questionnaire in my last letter. I hadn't. Not one jot or tittle of it.

Charity shop jigsaws are the best. For a puzzle of any kind to be a good puzzle it needs just the sort of extra ingredients that charity shop jigsaws frequently offer. For one thing, they may not be quite complete. So you are hunting for half a hand or the stalk of a tulip with the possibility – sounds like life! - that you may never find them. Though usually you do. With a greater sense of satisfaction than the foreseeable victories awaiting you in a puzzle from W.H. Smith, freshly unwrapped from its cellophane. And supposing there *are* missing pieces. Queen Victoria's nose. The prettiest rose in the cottage garden. There is the fun of deciding whether to get going with scissors, glue and felt tips to replace them or to chuck the whole lot away. If there's only one piece missing the decision is even harder. If there are, say, six, you shed few tears as you recycle them into the compost, feel pleased that you contributed £1.25 to helping the aged and look forward to another worthwhile find in due course. Another challenging characteristic is that sometimes the previous owner has collected all the edge pieces and put them in a separate bag. Dead set on giving the next puzzler a head start. A helping hand. Doing a lollipop lady on you. Nannying you gently into what is after all now *your* jigsaw and did you buy it just so that some meddling precursor should diminish your achievement and take away the pleasure of your own DIY triumph? No. Certainly not! (But you still have to deal with the moral debate, the temptation to, just for this once - excuse the split infinitive - tip out the edges from their bag and assemble them with frisky ease before tackling the 95% of middle bits.) With some puzzles, the lifting of the lid reveals great chunks of puzzle still locked alluringly together and you pray not to be led into the temptation of accepting, say, a wodge of pre-positioned boring sky pieces. The intriguing thing about a jigsaw – one of the 1000, or occasionally 2000 things – is that the moment it is finished it is completely without any interest whatsoever. In goes the last piece. Then it's 'how about a cup of tea?' Or, 'better do the weeding'. Whoosh, back goes the completed picture into the box, splurging into fragments, smithereens. As it should be. *Not* preserved, all done, behind glass, in a frame, in the manner of some practitioners, as if to say, look everyone, I put you together down to the very last piece, your magic is gone, your poison drawn, your power to baffle safely sealed up on the wall in the hall.

A neighbour recently presented me with a small tin of kudu paté. I had to look up kudu in the dictionary. It's a Hottentot word, the name of an African antelope with long spiral horns. The ingredients include port and brandy so I'm thinking of having it for supper, probably with a baguette. That seems more fitting than, say, a few slices of Waitrose cut white, since the Franck Food Cannery in Sebenza, South Africa, whence the paté came, "specialises in traditional French charcuterie." There's another tin for tomorrow: ostrich liver paté with green peppercorns.

On an extremely hot day last week, I encountered another neighbour for the first time. She lives in one of the flats further down the road. A Hungarian lady in her eighties who happened to announce that she liked my Bermuda shorts. She had evidently admired them as I negotiated the Pelican crossing at the bottom of Bressey Grove. Such a forthright comment on a first meeting quite obviously marked her out as someone I could get along with and enjoy knowing better. Though either her fashion sense or her eyesight may be seriously deficient. I put down my shopping. After twenty minutes or so of chat about the state of the world we agreed it would be nice if I went round for tea. Such an unusual woman. With stories to tell, she hinted, of narrow escapes from advancing armies and terrible losses and wartime tragedy. More of "a past" I suspect, than many people, but all perky and fragrantly elegant and alive in the present and looking forward to new experiences in the future. Including a cuppa with me!

August
An "on-board guide" is provided on trains nowadays.

An "on-board guide" is provided on trains nowadays. I glanced at one en route to Glasgow last week. It would probably have been helpful to include details of how to work the new-style press button lock toilets. I lost count of the number of times our peace and tranquillity was disturbed by a loud beeping sound because a toilet patron had pressed the alarm button instead of the lock release. My own visit lacked that sense of secure privacy that a visible lock ensures. So desirable on these occasions. Would the door suddenly spring open at the touch of an unseen hand? What I did read in the guide – and puzzle over – was that "Kylie Minogue's UK number one hit, 'Can't get you out of my head,' is the second most popular mobile phone ringtone download of all time!" Of course I admit that I don't have a clue what mobile phone ringtone downloads are. But can they, whatever they are, have been around for even a decade? All time? How long is *all time*?

Give me the patient unobtrusive pursuits of the trainspotters. No brash overstatements for them. No trumpeting. I observed them at intervals all along the route. Clapham Junction, Crewe, Wigan, Preston. Often alone, with notebook and modest holdall. Or 'holdlunch' perhaps. Not in anyone's way. Usually out at the end of the platform, far from any cosy buffets with steamed-up windows and the aroma of coffee. Waiting quietly in the teeth of any wind and vulnerable to passing showers to catch a glimpse of passing engines. Sometimes with a camera. Rarely if ever sitting down. Generally wearing sensible, appropriately waterproof clothing. Endearing really. Enviable even, in their quiet self-sufficiency. It's difficult to understand how anyone could find anything to mock in these placid hobbyists. Still less to fear from their relentlessly harmless activities. Passivities? But I read recently that "some rail companies are increasingly sure that terrorists may be disguising themselves as trainspotters." In a recent incident reported to Railway Magazine a spotter using a camera was told to leave a platform at Clapham Junction, the country's biggest interchange, after a member of staff told him he was breaching security. Others have alleged "various forms of unpleasant treatment, including being frogmarched from the platform and being yelled at over the public address system." The strange world of post September 11th.

On the tube the other day the driver wished to thank us for travelling on the Central Line and hoped we would have "a safe and happy day." It was probably a one-off. The notion that we would have been travelling on the Central Line if we had had a range of other options was, well, whimsical, to say the least. The one good thing about the announcement was that we heard it. On most stretches of the line the din of wheels on tracks precludes the possibility of picking up much of what any driver is saying. There are tantalising snippets of audibility like "…. station is closed so passengers should alight one stop earlier." No, to be fair, I have a lifelong affection for the underground trains. I go back to the steam trains that preceded them, when there were level crossings at all the local stations and nil chance of being electrocuted on the way to the Co-op. But don't tell anyone.

I was really annoyed with myself for forgetting to post my entry in the latest "Oldie" competition. You had to write a poem in praise of or anti breakfast. Every word in the first line had to begin with the same letter, with line two taking the next letter and so on. I was quite pleased with my opener:

"Awake! Athirst! Ah, apricots and ale, Aurora's appetites aroused again

Bravura breakfast, bloaters, brandy, brawn, bring beef by bucketfuls, bring brie!

Come, chosen chums, carouse companionably...." etc

Still, I didn't begrudge the first prize to

"Bed. Bliss. Blast! Bettina brings

Crummy croissants, cornflakes, clattering cups...." etc

No use whining over spilt milk or throwing stones after the horse has bolted. We all know a stitch in time gathers no moss. One of my father's office colleagues used to specialise in mixed metaphors. Pig in a silk purse. Out of the frying pan into the china shop. That sort of thing. After a business trip he was always pleased, when his plane landed, to "get his feet back on terra cotta."

November
Planes queue outside my bedroom window

Planes queue outside my bedroom window. Not jostling exactly, like on the first day of Harrods' sale. But definitely queuing. At 6.30 yesterday morning I watched five airliners glide round quietly within five minutes, into their "slot" en route to Heathrow. I could picture the screens clocking up the welcome news to waiting friends and families: "On approach." Saturday morning is particularly popular for a stream of very early morning arrivals. Presumably after transatlantic night flights. Exactly where they come from I don't know; where they are going, I do. I must be a real townie. My imagination is more fired by planes than by birds. Round here we mainly do jays and magpies, pigeons and robins with the odd blackbird thrown in. But you do see plenty of birds in those fast-moving arrow-head formation flights from my window as well. The sky seems to belong to them. Effortless concord. Like the planes, they too always appear to have a fixed destination in mind. Do they take it in turns to lead, while the rest slipstream, like in the Tour de France? Avian transworld tourists, as opposed to "Won't be long, dear. Just popping out for a worm." Considering how uncluttered it is, there is really quite a lot going on in the sky. Clouds. Jumbo jets. Weather. On my last trip to Bristol, Mary and I attended a kite festival. One of her former pupils won second prize in the prestigious all-comers National Kite-Flying Championships. The miracle was that anyone got a kite up into the sky at all. After a gloriously appropriate windy week, there was a flat calm that day and expertise with wrist-work rather than exploitation of air currents was what sorted out the men from the boys. There is evidently a complete competitive kite-flying language every bit as complex as in, say, international figure skating with its triple salchows and double axels and what have you. One technique involves manoeuvring the kite so that it swoops down and bounces along the turf on one of its points before soaring skyward again. Thrilling. But it's not all, or even most of the time, an experience of elemental ecstasy, this kite-flying business. All over the vast competition site lone aspirants sat patiently, painstakingly, disentangling knots from their lines in preparation for their next attempt. When the moment comes, off you go, sprinting across the field, eyes skyward, arms flailing, everything you've got in the way of mental and physical strength dedicated to keeping that fragile flyer hovering tentatively overhead for a few more triumphant moments. We strolled home across the suspension bridge and had a mug of tea in lazy armchairs.

A week or so later, when I happened to be in South Woodford library checking up on a quotation for my Enigma Crossword, I asked the librarian for the Dewey reference number for kite-flying. For the next ten minutes at least I was belting round the library in his wake, beads of enthusiastic perspiration on his brow. "Please, don't let me keep you from whatever it was you were busy with." Smiling response: "Oh, don't mention it; this is much more exciting!"(Exciting! Hunting down books on kites?)

"The only place we'll find kites is in the Junior Library," jumping down the steps two at a time to that section of the building. "Yes! Here we are: *Making and Flying stunt Kites* by Wolfgang Schimmelpfennig."

W.S. included instructions on how to make the patchwork three-stick hexagonal kite. He also included in his brief history of kite-flying the intriguing fact that during the First World War a Chief Kite Instructor was appointed to the British War Office. But by this time my sprinting accomplice was heading off towards the Reference shelves upstairs. "Ah! I thought so. Bound to be something in here! *A Comprehensive Encyclopaedia of Sport.*"

But there was nothing on kite-flying. Only "kite-fighting." In Thailand – you never know when this information may be useful – the kite-fighting season extends from February to June. Trophies attract hot competition from the popular kite-flying leagues. One competition involves the large star-shaped male kite, the *chula,* battling it out with two much smaller diamond-shaped female kites, the *pakpaos.* The chula has bamboo slats in its tail with which it tries to entangle the tail of a pakpao. Meanwhile the pakpaos gang up and try to catch one of the points of the chula star in carefully positioned loops, to bring it down. Kite-fighting has been popular for centuries in Japan where sometimes the kites are as big as 1000 square feet and need the entire population of the village to launch them. A lot healthier than bingo in my view.

I have been told to be sure to include details of tea with my new octogenarian friend from Eastern Europe. She continues to surprise. I get clear instructions when I visit: "Bring two Danish pastries, darling." I generally seem to hit on the day when she has "had the hairdresser round." Last time I went she said I was probably wondering why she still had all her rollers in. I wasn't and said so. It's a free country after all. "The curls stay in better if I leave the rollers in longer." All the furniture was covered in dust-sheets, as she was expecting the decorators. Her name is Iby. She has a baby grand piano and speaks six languages. Fancy meeting her at the pelican crossing! Iby was attending to her eyebrows while we talked. "I have a new partner this evening!" she confided. My admiration soared! "His usual partner is on holiday in Jersey. We're playing at Gants Hill Club for a change." Iby again had her rollers in when we took a drive through the forest out to Epping for tea a fortnight ago. But they were hidden under a kind of turban, creamy-coloured, and she looked as striking as ever. We tried "The Thatched House" but it was very noisy and beery with no sign of teapots so we opted for Poppy's Coffee and Tea Rooms across the main road. "I just hold up my hand and smile and the cars usually stop for me," she remarked, over her shoulder in mid traffic. Iby's husband died years ago. Twenty years or so. "We were very happy, darling. We argued all the time." She visits his grave each week and talks with him. Argues probably, only it must be disappointingly one-sided. And she loves chocolate. When I opened her fridge to get the milk it was all I could see. My first joyous impressions of Iby were correct! "We're alive, you and I," she sometimes says.

I don't visit Alastair's grave in Scotland. But every day holds reminders of his familiar sayings. "We live under one another's forgiveness": that was one of his most cherished precepts. Returning from that kite festival weekend in Bristol, I could hardly miss – no-one could – a massive white painted message high up on a steep hillside bordering the motorway in enormous perfectly formed capital letters: "ALICE, SORRY." Visible for miles to all who passed by. And crucially, I suppose, to Alice. It was impossible to be unmoved by this anonymous penitent - or vandal, according to viewpoint. Someone evidently with considerable energy, possibly born of desperation if so colossal an apology were

170

called for. Did he have brush-wielding accomplices? Was it all done during one night? I hope Alice has forgiven him. Or her?

I am gradually covering the breakfast room wall with "still lifes." It takes time. A print or two from the National Gallery. Some picked up from charity shops. There was a time when it seemed wholly inexplicable to me that anyone should settle down with brushes and paints and dedicated concentration to compose and execute a picture of a kettle. Or maybe a few old pots, bottles, plates. Cracked ones even. However nicely arranged. I could understand why people painted people. And celebrations of historic or mythical events were self-evidently worth recording on canvas. But it was harder to grasp the allure as subject-matter of a random collection of items that might pass unnoticed in an average kitchen or garden shed. Sometimes I assumed that artists were just making sensible use of something near at hand to practise on. Sometimes I even got so far as to wonder whether artists took pity on the humble pots and pans, rather like Gray who wanted to celebrate his little flower "born to blush unseen and waste its sweetness on the desert air." I can't really pinpoint the moment when I saw the light. Who knows? Perhaps I'm still in the dark! But it could be that those strange seven years of our confinement at home together enabled me to look at the extraordinary value of ordinary, unremarkable things. Things for which familiarity hadn't bred contempt, but merely lack of awareness. There are probably a great many things that I "see" differently these days. Things like walking. Getting up and sitting down. Quiet conversation between clear and equal minds. Even flower pots, and kettles.

Phoebe is wanting her Whiskas. I'm looking after her for next door. Must go.

171